Frankenstein

THE GRAPHIC NOVEL
Mary Shelley

Script by Jason Cobley
Adapted by Brigit Viney

HEINLE
CENGAGE Learning

Australia • Brazil • Japan • Korea • Mexico • Singapore • Spain • United Kingdom • United States

HEINLE
CENGAGE Learning™

Frankenstein: The Graphic Novel
Mary Shelley
Script by Jason Cobley
Adapted by Brigit Viney

Publisher: Sherrise Roehr

Editor in Chief: Clive Bryant

Development Editors: John Hicks
and Jennifer Nunan

Contributing Writer: Amanda Cole

Director of Global Marketing:
Ian Martin

Director of U.S. Marketing:
Jim McDonough

Content Project Manager:
Natalie Griffith

Senior Print Buyer: Mary Beth
Hennebury

Cover / Text Designer: Jo Wheeler

Compositor: Jo Wheeler,
Jenny Placentino, and
Macmillan Publishing Solutions

Art Director: Jon Haward

Linework: Declan Shalvey

Coloring: Jason Cardy and
Kat Nicholson

Lettering: Terry Wiley

Audio: EFS Television Production Ltd.

ISBN-13: 978-1-4240-3184-9

ISBN-10: 1-4240-3184-2

Heinle
20 Channel Center Street
Boston, MA 02210
USA

Cengage Learning is a leading provider of customized learning
solutions with office locations around the globe, including Singapore,
the United Kingdom, Australia, Mexico, Brazil, and Japan. Locate your
local office at **www.cengage.com/global**

Cengage Learning products are represented in Canada by
Nelson Education, Ltd.

Visit Heinle online at **elt.heinle.com**

Visit our corporate website at **www.cengage.com**

Published in association with Classical Comics Ltd.

Printed in Mexico
8 16 15

Contents

Characters

Victor Frankenstein

Frankenstein's Monster

Elizabeth Lavenza
Victor's adopted sister

Robert Walton
Adventurer

The Ship's Master

The Ship's Officer

Alphonse Frankenstein
Victor's father

Caroline Frankenstein
Victor's mother

Ernest Frankenstein
Victor's brother

William Frankenstein
Victor's brother

Henry Clerval
Victor's friend

Justine Moritz
Servant to Frankenstein's family

Characters

Monsieur Krempe
*Professor of Natural Science,
Ingolstadt University*

Monsieur Waldman
*Professor of Chemistry,
Ingolstadt University*

Lawyer
*States the charge against
Justine Moritz*

Old Woman
*Gives evidence against
Justine Mortiz*

Monsieur De Lacey
Peasant

Agatha De Lacey
*Peasant, daughter of
Monsieur De Lacey*

Felix De Lacey
*Peasant, son of
Monsieur De Lacey*

Turkish Merchant

Safie
Daughter of the Turkish Merchant

Mr. Kirwin
Magistrate

Fisherman

Judge in Geneva

Introduction

Mary Shelley's classic novel, *Frankenstein,* was first published in 1818. It was written in the days before steam travel, when the world seemed much bigger than it does today. Only the bravest adventurers could visit distant places and discover the secrets they held. It was possible that there could be things — things created by humans — that would terrify anyone who saw them.

Science was progressing extremely quickly, and it seemed that anything and everything was possible as humans found new and powerful ways to create and to destroy.

At the same time, medicine was finding new ways to cure sick people and to make people live longer. This raised questions about the nature of life itself. For example, if a dying man could be saved and brought back to life, could a dead man also be brought back to life? What about a dead person made from parts of other dead people? Could a creature like that be given life as well?

Where would it end? Would it go too far?

Indeed, in the early days of scientific advances, anything and everything seemed possible ...

NEAR THE COAST OF RUSSIA ...
FROM THE LETTERS OF ROBERT WALTON:

LETTER 1 - DECEMBER 11, 17--

MY DEAR SISTER,
I AM ALREADY FAR FROM LONDON.
THE COLD NORTHERN WIND ON MY FACE
FILLS ME WITH HAPPINESS. IT GIVES ME
A TASTE OF THE WONDERFUL PLACE I
AM GOING TO. AT THE NORTH POLE,
MARGARET, THE SUN IS ALWAYS IN THE
SKY. IT IS A LAND OF BEAUTY AND
AMAZING SIGHTS.

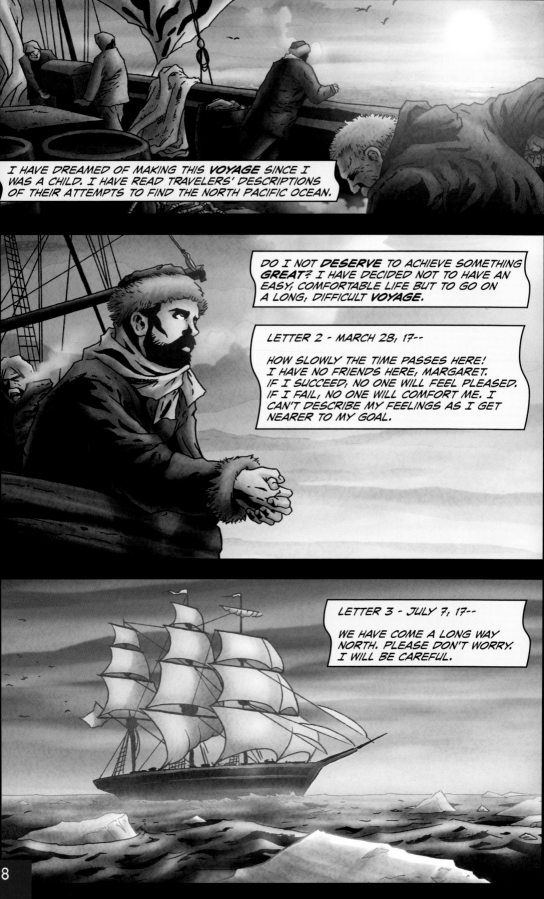

I HAVE DREAMED OF MAKING THIS **VOYAGE** SINCE I WAS A CHILD. I HAVE READ TRAVELERS' DESCRIPTIONS OF THEIR ATTEMPTS TO FIND THE NORTH PACIFIC OCEAN.

DO I NOT **DESERVE** TO ACHIEVE SOMETHING **GREAT**? I HAVE DECIDED NOT TO HAVE AN EASY, COMFORTABLE LIFE BUT TO GO ON A LONG, DIFFICULT **VOYAGE**.

LETTER 2 - MARCH 28, 17--

HOW SLOWLY THE TIME PASSES HERE! I HAVE NO FRIENDS HERE, MARGARET. IF I SUCCEED, NO ONE WILL FEEL PLEASED. IF I FAIL, NO ONE WILL COMFORT ME. I CAN'T DESCRIBE MY FEELINGS AS I GET NEARER TO MY GOAL.

LETTER 3 - JULY 7, 17--

WE HAVE COME A LONG WAY NORTH. PLEASE DON'T WORRY. I WILL BE CAREFUL.

LETTER 4 - AUGUST 5, 17--

LAST MONDAY, THE SHIP WAS NEARLY **SURROUNDED** BY ICE, AND THERE WAS A VERY THICK FOG. WE DECIDED TO STOP MOVING AND TO WAIT FOR A CHANGE IN THE WEATHER.

AT TWO O'CLOCK, THE FOG DISAPPEARED, AND THERE WAS ICE EVERYWHERE – AS FAR AS WE COULD SEE. WE WERE WORRIED; AND THEN, IN THE DISTANCE, WE SAW SOMETHING STRANGE.

IT WAS A **SLED** ABOUT HALF A MILE AWAY. A HUGE MAN WAS DRIVING IT. WE WERE AMAZED TO SEE SOMEONE SO FAR FROM LAND. WE WERE UNABLE TO FOLLOW HIM BECAUSE WE WERE STUCK IN THE ICE.

THE NEXT MORNING WHEN I WOKE UP, ALL THE SAILORS WERE TALKING TO SOMEONE IN THE SEA. IT WAS, IN FACT, A SIMILAR **SLED**, WHICH HAD COME TOWARD US IN THE NIGHT ON A LARGE PIECE OF ICE. THE MAN ABOARD WAS NOT HUGE LIKE THE OTHER TRAVELER, BUT A **EUROPEAN**. THE SAILORS WERE **PERSUADING** HIM TO COME ONTO THE SHIP.

HERE IS OUR **CAPTAIN**, AND HE WON'T LET YOU DIE OUT ON THE ICE.

COULD YOU TELL ME WHERE YOU'RE GOING?

WE'RE ON A **VOYAGE** OF DISCOVERY TO THE NORTH POLE.

WHEN HE HEARD THIS, HE AGREED TO COME ON **BOARD**.

HE WAS NEARLY **FROZEN** AND EXTREMELY THIN. I HAVE NEVER SEEN A MAN IN SUCH A TERRIBLE STATE. SLOWLY, WE HELPED HIM **RECOVER**. TWO DAYS PASSED BEFORE HE WAS ABLE TO SPEAK.

WHY DID YOU COME SO FAR ON THE ICE?

I WAS LOOKING FOR SOMEONE WHO HAD RUN AWAY FROM ME.

I THINK WE'VE SEEN HIM.

WE SAW A MAN ON A **SLED**. SOME DOGS WERE PULLING IT ACROSS THE ICE.

DO YOU THINK THAT WHEN THE ICE BROKE IT DESTROYED HIS **SLED**?

THE ICE DIDN'T BREAK UNTIL NEARLY MIDNIGHT. HE WAS PROBABLY SAFE BY THEN.

I'M SURE YOU WANT TO ASK ME A LOT OF QUESTIONS. YOU SAVED ME AND HAVE BROUGHT ME BACK TO LIFE!

THE STRANGER SUDDENLY SEEMED MORE ALIVE.

AUGUST 13, 17--

I LIKE MY GUEST MORE AND MORE EACH DAY. I ADMIRE HIM AND ALSO FEEL SORRY FOR HIM. HE HAS NOW **RECOVERED** FROM HIS ILLNESS.

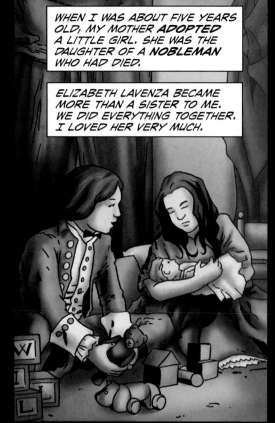

FOR SEVERAL YEARS, I WAS THEIR ONLY CHILD. THEY LOVED ME DEEPLY.

WHEN I WAS ABOUT FIVE YEARS OLD, MY MOTHER **ADOPTED** A LITTLE GIRL. SHE WAS THE DAUGHTER OF A **NOBLEMAN** WHO HAD DIED.

ELIZABETH LAVENZA BECAME MORE THAN A SISTER TO ME. WE DID EVERYTHING TOGETHER. I LOVED HER VERY MUCH.

VOLUME I
CHAPTER II

WE WERE BROUGHT UP TOGETHER. THERE WAS LESS THAN A YEAR BETWEEN OUR AGES.

WHEN MY PARENTS HAD ANOTHER SON, WE WENT BACK TO GENEVA AND SETTLED THERE.

IN GENEVA, I BECAME CLOSE FRIENDS WITH HENRY CLERVAL. HE LOVED READING AND WRITING STORIES.

ELIZABETH WAS KIND AND LOVING. SHE SHOWED CLERVAL THE BEAUTY OF GOODNESS.

I READ WITH **GREAT PLEASURE** THE WORKS OF MEN WHO HAD STUDIED NATURE AND DISCOVERED ITS SECRETS.

I BECAME THEIR FOLLOWER. I DIDN'T WANT MONEY, BUT I WANTED THE **GLORY** OF A **GREAT** DISCOVERY.

I WANTED TO FREE PEOPLE FROM **DISEASE**.

WHEN I WAS FIFTEEN, I **WITNESSED** A TERRIBLE STORM.

THE *THUNDER* WAS FRIGHTENINGLY LOUD.

CRACK!

AS I WATCHED THE STORM, A *STREAM* OF FIRE SUDDENLY CAME OUT OF AN OLD TREE NEAR OUR HOUSE.

WHEN THE FIRE DIED OUT, MOST OF THE TREE HAD DISAPPEARED.

THE NEXT MORNING, WE FOUND THAT THE BOTTOM OF THE TREE HAD BEEN BROKEN INTO LONG, THIN PIECES. I BECAME INTERESTED IN ELECTRICITY; AND I BEGAN TO STUDY MATHEMATICS AND OTHER SCIENCES.

BUT **DESTINY** WAS TOO POWERFUL. SHE HAD ALREADY DECIDED ON MY DESTRUCTION.

VOLUME I
CHAPTER III

WHEN I WAS SEVENTEEN, MY PARENTS DECIDED TO SEND ME TO INGOLSTADT UNIVERSITY.

THEN ELIZABETH BECAME VERY SICK. MY MOTHER TOOK CARE OF HER, AND ELIZABETH **RECOVERED**. HOWEVER, THEN MY MOTHER BECAME SICK.

My children, I always wanted you to marry each other.

Elizabeth, my love, you must be a mother to my younger children.

I'm sad that I have to leave you, but I will try to accept death cheerfully.

I hope to see you in another world.

SHE DIED CALMLY.

MY MOTHER WAS **DEAD** -

- BUT WE STILL HAD DUTIES TO PERFORM. ELIZABETH HID HER **SORROW** AND TRIED TO COMFORT US ALL.

FINALLY, THE DAY CAME WHEN I HAD TO GO TO INGOLSTADT.

WRITE OFTEN, VICTOR.

I LOVED MY BROTHERS, ELIZABETH, AND CLERVAL, BUT I **LONGED** TO ACQUIRE KNOWLEDGE.

17

AFTER A LONG, TIRING JOURNEY, I ARRIVED AT INGOLSTADT.

THE NEXT MORNING, I DELIVERED MY LETTERS OF INTRODUCTION.

CHANCE LED ME FIRST TO ...

VOLUME I
CHAPTER IV

I FOUND A TRUE FRIEND IN **MONSIEUR** WALDMAN.

HE SMOOTHED THE PATH OF KNOWLEDGE FOR ME IN A THOUSAND WAYS. IN THE NEXT TWO YEARS, MY DISCOVERIES MADE ME WELL RESPECTED AT THE UNIVERSITY.

I WAS ESPECIALLY INTERESTED IN ANYTHING THAT LIVED. I WANTED TO KNOW WHERE LIFE CAME FROM.

TO EXAMINE THE CAUSES OF LIFE, WE MUST FIRST EXAMINE DEATH.

I WANTED TO SEE WHAT HAPPENS TO THE BODY AFTER DEATH.

TO ME, A **GRAVEYARD** WAS JUST A PLACE THAT WAS FULL OF **DEAD** BODIES. I WASN'T AFRAID OF IT.

FOR DAYS AND NIGHTS, I EXAMINED **DEAD** BODIES AND HOW THEY **DECAYED**.

THEN SUDDENLY, AFTER WEEKS OF EXTREMELY HARD WORK ...

... I SUCCEEDED IN DISCOVERING THE CAUSE OF LIFE!

FOR A LONG TIME, I WASN'T SURE HOW TO USE THIS *ASTONISHING* POWER.

I WAS ABLE TO CREATE LIFE ...

... BUT TO MAKE A BODY REMAINED EXTREMELY DIFFICULT.

THE SMALLNESS OF MANY PARTS OF THE BODY MADE MY WORK VERY SLOW, SO I DECIDED TO MAKE THE BODY LARGER THAN NORMAL – ABOUT EIGHT FEET TALL.

MAKING THIS BODY WAS ALL I COULD THINK ABOUT.

ALONE IN MY ROOM, I WORKED ON MY CREATION.

OFTEN, I HATED WHAT I WAS DOING.

I WORKED SO HARD THAT I BECAME SICK AND VERY NERVOUS. I COULDN'T SPEAK TO ANYONE.

21

VOLUME I
CHAPTER V

ON A DARK
EVENING IN
NOVEMBER,
I FINALLY
FINISHED.

I PREPARED TO PUT LIFE
INTO THE LIFELESS THING.

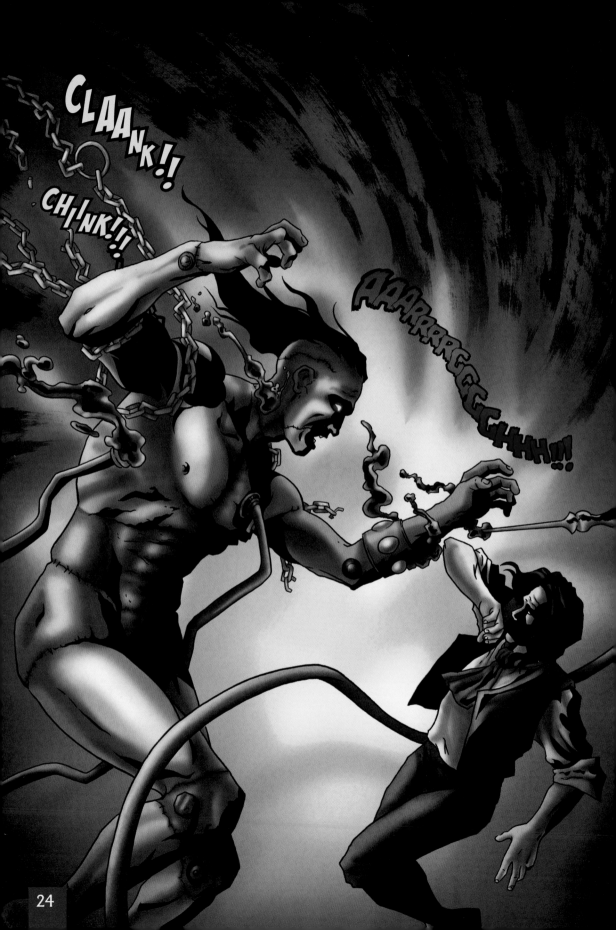

I DREAMED ABOUT ELIZABETH. SHE WAS WALKING IN INGOLSTADT.

PLEASED AND SURPRISED, I *EMBRACED* HER ...

... BUT AS I KISSED HER LIPS ...

... THEY TURNED DEATHLY WHITE ...

I SAW THE **MONSTER** THAT I HAD CREATED.

UNGHH ... MUH ...

PERHAPS HE SPOKE, BUT I DIDN'T HEAR.

ONE HAND REACHED OUT TO STOP ME, BUT I ESCAPED ...

... AND RAN INTO THE **COURTYARD**. I STAYED THERE ALL NIGHT. ALL THE TIME I WAS LISTENING FOR THE SOUND OF THE **MONSTER**.

HIS **UGLINESS** WAS INCREDIBLE. WHAT I HAD DREAMED OF HAD BECOME MY **HELL**.

WHEN MORNING CAME, I WANTED TO AVOID THE *MONSTER*.

I DID NOT DARE RETURN TO MY APARTMENT, SO I WALKED AROUND THE TOWN.

I DIDN'T KNOW WHERE I WAS OR WHAT I WAS DOING.

MY HEART *BEAT* HARD WITH FEAR.

MY DEAR FRANKENSTEIN!

I'M SO PLEASED TO SEE YOU!

I WAS SHAKING NERVOUSLY AS WE WALKED TO MY COLLEGE.

I THOUGHT THE CREATURE COULD STILL BE IN MY APARTMENT.

I WAS AFRAID TO SEE HIM BUT EVEN MORE AFRAID THAT HENRY WOULD SEE HIM.

HENRY, WAIT HERE FOR A FEW MINUTES.

I FELT COLD WITH FEAR ...

... BUT I SAW THAT MY ENEMY HAD GONE.

I CLAPPED MY HANDS FOR JOY AND RAN DOWN FOR HENRY.

THE **SERVANT** BROUGHT US BREAKFAST, BUT I WAS TOO EXCITED TO EAT.

HA HA HA HA!

HA-HA HA HA-HAH!!!

HA-HARRH!

VICTOR!

WHAT'S THE MATTER?

WHAT'S MAKING YOU LIKE THIS?

I THOUGHT I HAD SEEN THE **MONSTER** IN MY ROOM.

HE CAN TELL YOU!

DEAR VICTOR,

YOU HAVE BEEN SICK, VERY SICK, AND I AM WORRIED ABOUT YOU.

GET WELL AND COME HOME. YOUR FATHER REALLY WANTS TO SEE YOU.

ERNEST IS SIXTEEN NOW. HE WANTS VERY MUCH TO GO ABROAD, BUT WE CAN'T LET HIM LEAVE UNTIL YOU COME HOME.

AND LITTLE WILLIAM IS LOVELY. HE IS VERY TALL FOR HIS AGE AND SMILES AND LAUGHS A LOT. HE ALREADY HAS TWO LITTLE "WIVES"! LOUISA IS HIS FAVORITE. SHE'S FIVE.

DO YOU REMEMBER OUR **SERVANT** JUSTINE MORITZ? HER MOTHER TREATED HER BADLY, SO SHE CAME TO US WHEN SHE WAS TWELVE.

YOU LIKED HER VERY MUCH. SHE COULD ALWAYS MAKE YOU FEEL HAPPY.

ONE BY ONE, HER BROTHERS AND SISTER DIED, AND HER MOTHER CALLED HER HOME. SOMETIMES HER MOTHER WAS SORRY FOR WHAT SHE HAD DONE. AT OTHER TIMES, SHE SAID THAT JUSTINE HAD CAUSED THE DEATHS OF HER BROTHERS AND SISTER.

BUT NOW HER MOTHER IS AT PEACE: SHE DIED AT THE BEGINNING OF LAST WINTER.

JUSTINE HAS COME BACK TO US, AND I LOVE HER DEARLY. SHE IS CLEVER, GENTLE, AND VERY PRETTY.

I FEEL BETTER NOW BECAUSE I HAVE WRITTEN TO YOU, DEAR VICTOR. GOOD-BYE! AND PLEASE WRITE TO ME.

ELIZABETH LAVENZA

DEAR, DEAR ELIZABETH! I WILL WRITE IMMEDIATELY!

I WROTE AND FELT VERY TIRED, BUT IT WAS THE START OF MY RECOVERY. TWO WEEKS LATER, I WAS WELL ENOUGH TO LEAVE MY ROOM.

I HATED NATURAL SCIENCE AND THE SIGHT OF MY SCIENTIFIC EQUIPMENT. I COULD NEVER TELL HENRY ABOUT WHAT I HAD DONE OR WHAT HAD HAPPENED ON THAT TERRIBLE NIGHT.

HENRY HAD COME TO THE UNIVERSITY TO STUDY THE LANGUAGES OF THE EAST, AND I BEGAN TO STUDY THEM WITH HIM.

I FOUND COMFORT IN THE WRITINGS OF THE EASTERN *POETS*.

THEY WROTE ABOUT A WARM SUN AND GARDENS, AN *ENEMY* WHO BEHAVES WELL, AND THE FIRE THAT BURNS IN YOUR OWN HEART.

SUMMER PASSED, AND WINTER CAME. I WANTED TO GO BACK TO GENEVA, BUT THERE WAS TOO MUCH SNOW. SPRING CAME AGAIN.

HENRY SUGGESTED THAT WE GO WALKING AROUND INGOLSTADT BEFORE WE RETURNED TO GENEVA.

WHAT AN EXCELLENT FRIEND!

FOR TWO WEEKS, WE WALKED IN THE COUNTRYSIDE. HENRY TAUGHT ME TO LOVE NATURE AGAIN AND THE HAPPY FACES OF CHILDREN.

I FELT VERY HAPPY AND HAD NO WORRIES AT ALL.

BLAC

WHEN I RETURNED TO INGOLSTADT, I FOUND THIS LETTER FROM MY FATHER.

MY DEAR VICTOR,

YOU HAVE PROBABLY WAITED FOR A LETTER SO THAT YOU CAN ARRANGE THE DATE OF YOUR RETURN. SO HOW CAN I TELL YOU ABOUT WHAT HAS HAPPENED TO US?

WILLIAM IS **DEAD**! THAT SWEET CHILD WHO WAS SO GENTLE! VICTOR – SOMEONE HAS MURDERED HIM!

LAST THURSDAY, WE ALL WENT FOR A WALK IN PLAINPALAIS. IT WAS A BEAUTIFUL, WARM EVENING, AND WE WENT FARTHER THAN USUAL.

ERNEST! WILLIAM!

IT WAS GETTING DARK WHEN WE DECIDED TO TURN BACK. WILLIAM AND ERNEST HAD GONE AHEAD OF US, SO WE CALLED FOR THEM.

HAVE YOU SEEN WILLIAM?

WE WERE PLAYING, AND HE RAN AWAY TO HIDE.

I TRIED TO FIND HIM AND WAITED FOR HIM, BUT HE HASN'T COME BACK!

WE SEARCHED FOR HIM ALL NIGHT.

I COULDN'T REST WHILE HE WAS LOST.

AT ABOUT FIVE IN THE MORNING, I DISCOVERED MY LOVELY BOY, **PALE** AND STILL.

THE **MARKS** OF THE MURDERER'S FINGERS WERE ON HIS NECK.

OH, GOD! I'VE MURDERED HIM!

I LET HIM WEAR A VALUABLE PICTURE OF YOUR MOTHER AROUND HIS NECK. IT'S GONE. IT MUST BE THE REASON SOMEONE KILLED HIM.

WE ARE DOING EVERYTHING WE CAN TO FIND THE MURDERER, BUT THAT WON'T BRING BACK MY DEAREST WILLIAM.

41

COME HOME, DEAREST VICTOR. ONLY YOU CAN COMFORT ELIZABETH. SHE CRIES ALL THE TIME AND **BLAMES** HERSELF FOR WILLIAM'S DEATH. WILL YOU RETURN AND COMFORT US ALL?

YOUR LOVING FATHER, ALPHONSE FRANKENSTEIN

MY DEAR FRANKENSTEIN, THIS IS TERRIBLE NEWS. WHAT ARE YOU GOING TO DO?

I'M GOING TO GENEVA IMMEDIATELY.

I SAID GOOD-BYE TO MY FRIEND. AS I GOT CLOSER TO HOME, I FELT TERRIBLY SAD AND AFRAID.

AS I SAID THESE WORDS, I SAW A FIGURE IN THE DARKNESS.

A *FLASH* OF *LIGHTNING* SHOWED ME WHO IT WAS ...

... THE *DEVIL* THAT I HAD CREATED.

WHAT WAS HE DOING THERE? COULD HE BE THE MURDERER OF MY BROTHER?

I BECAME SURE THAT HE WAS.

HE WAS THE MURDERER!

WHEN I SAW HIM AGAIN; HE WAS AMONG THE ROCKS NEAR THE TOP OF THE MOUNTAIN.

HE SOON REACHED THE TOP ...

... AND DISAPPEARED.

IT WAS ABOUT FIVE IN THE MORNING WHEN I ARRIVED AT MY FATHER'S HOUSE.

I TOLD THE **SERVANTS** NOT TO WAKE THE FAMILY, AND I WENT INTO THE LIBRARY.

SIX YEARS HAD PASSED SINCE I LEFT.

Caroline Beaufort-Frankens

MY DEAREST VICTOR!

ERNEST!

AH! THIS IS SUCH A SAD TIME ...

... BUT I'M SURE YOU WILL BE ABLE TO HELP OUR FATHER AND ELIZABETH.

ELIZABETH?

SHE NEEDS COMFORT THE MOST.

SHE **BLAMES** HERSELF FOR WILLIAM'S MURDER.

BUT NOW WE HAVE FOUND THE MURDERER.

PAPA! VICTOR SAYS HE KNOWS THE MURDERER! HE SAYS JUSTINE IS **INNOCENT!**

IF SHE IS, I HOPE THE COURT DOES NOT DECIDE SHE IS **GUILTY.**

YOUR ARRIVAL, VICTOR, FILLS ME WITH HOPE. I WILL NEVER BE HAPPY AGAIN IF JUSTINE DIES.

SHE IS **INNOCENT.** DON'T BE AFRAID.

VOLUME I
CHAPTER VIII

WE SPENT A FEW SAD HOURS TOGETHER UNTIL WE WENT TO THE **TRIAL.**

WHEN JUSTINE CAME INTO THE COURT, SHE LOOKED CALM AND CONFIDENT.

SHE LOOKED AT US LOVINGLY.

JUSTINE HAD BEEN OUT ON THE NIGHT OF THE MURDER. EARLY THE NEXT MORNING, A WOMAN WHO WORKS AT THE MARKET SAW HER NEAR THE PLACE WHERE WILLIAM'S BODY WAS FOUND.

JUSTINE WAS CALLED TO DEFEND HERSELF. AT TIMES, SHE ALMOST CRIED, BUT SHE SPOKE CLEARLY.

I ASKED HER WHAT SHE WAS DOING. SHE GAVE ME A CONFUSED ANSWER.

GOD KNOWS THAT I AM COMPLETELY **INNOCENT**.

I SPENT THE EVENING AT MY AUNT'S HOUSE.

ON MY WAY HOME, A MAN ASKED ME IF I HAD SEEN THE CHILD WHO WAS LOST.

I SPENT MANY HOURS LOOKING FOR HIM. WHEN I TRIED TO RETURN TO GENEVA, THE GATES WERE SHUT. I HAD TO SPEND THE NIGHT IN A **BARN**.

THIS IS THE PICTURE THAT THE **SERVANT** FOUND IN JUSTINE'S POCKET.

ELIZABETH HAD PLACED IT AROUND WILLIAM'S NECK BEFORE HE DISAPPEARED.

A SOUND OF **HORROR** AND ANGER FILLED THE COURT.

IN THE EARLY MORNING, THE SOUND OF **FOOTSTEPS** WOKE ME. I DECIDED TO LOOK FOR THE MISSING CHILD AGAIN.

I WAS VERY TIRED WHEN I MET THE MARKET WOMAN BECAUSE I HADN'T SLEPT MUCH.

I DON'T KNOW HOW THE PICTURE GOT IN MY POCKET. I CAN'T EXPLAIN IT.

THE COURT MUST DECIDE NOW WHAT HAPPENS TO ME.

ALTHOUGH ELIZABETH AND OTHERS SPOKE WELL OF JUSTINE, PEOPLE IN THE COURT WERE ANGRY WITH HER.

THE NEXT MORNING, I WENT TO THE COURT. THEY DECIDED JUSTINE WAS **GUILTY**.

... BUT SHE HAS **CONFESSED!**

HOW WILL I EVER BELIEVE AGAIN IN HUMAN GOODNESS?

I WILL SEE HER ALTHOUGH SHE IS **GUILTY**, AND YOU MUST COME WITH ME, VICTOR.

OH, JUSTINE!

I THOUGHT YOU WERE **INNOCENT!**

I **CONFESSED**, BUT I LIED. I AM **INNOCENT!**

OH, JUSTINE! **FORGIVE** ME FOR NOT TRUSTING YOU.

DO NOT FEAR - I'LL **PROVE** YOU'RE **INNOCENT.**

YOU WILL NOT DIE!

I'M NOT AFRAID TO DIE.

I CAN DIE IN PEACE NOW THAT YOU AND YOUR FAMILY KNOW I'M **INNOCENT.**

THE POOR SUFFERER TRIED TO COMFORT US ALL. BUT I, THE TRUE MURDERER, COULD NOT FEEL COMFORTED.

THE NEXT MORNING, JUSTINE DIED.

THOSE I LOVED CRIED OVER THE **GRAVES** OF WILLIAM AND JUSTINE – THE FIRST **VICTIMS** OF MY CREATION.

MY FATHER'S HEALTH WAS SHAKEN, AND ELIZABETH WAS VERY SAD. I FELT DEEPLY TROUBLED. ONE DAY, I SUDDENLY DECIDED TO LEAVE.

VOLUME II
CHAPTER I

I HAD WANTED TO HELP OTHER PEOPLE, BUT NOW EVERYTHING WAS RUINED. FULL OF **GUILT**, I NEEDED TO BE ALONE.

I HAD CAUSED SOME TERRIBLE **EVILS**, AND I WAS VERY AFRAID THAT THE **MONSTER** WOULD DO SOMETHING ELSE.

I WENT TO THE **ALPINE** VALLEYS BECAUSE I THOUGHT I COULD FORGET MY **SORROWS** THERE. AFTER A TIME, I ARRIVED AT THE VILLAGE OF CHAMONIX.

VOLUME II
CHAPTER II

I DECIDED TO CLIMB TO THE TOP OF MONTANVERT. I REMEMBERED THE VIEW FROM THE TOP. IT HAD HAD A **GREAT** EFFECT ON ME WHEN I FIRST SAW IT.

THE CLIMB WAS DANGEROUS. THE TOPS OF THE MOUNTAINS WERE HIDDEN IN CLOUDS, AND RAIN FELL HEAVILY FROM THE DARK SKY.

IT WAS NEARLY NOON WHEN I ARRIVED AT THE TOP OF THE MOUNTAIN. I SAT ON A ROCK AND LOOKED AT THE WONDERFUL VIEW.

MY HEART FILLED WITH JOY.

ALLOW ME THIS HAPPINESS OR TAKE ME AWAY FROM THE JOYS OF LIFE!

AS I SAID THIS, I SUDDENLY SAW THE FIGURE OF A HUGE MAN. HE WAS COMING TOWARD ME AT **GREAT** SPEED.

IT WAS THE **MONSTER** THAT I HAD CREATED. I SHOOK WITH ANGER AND **HORROR**. I WANTED TO FIGHT HIM AND TO KILL HIM!

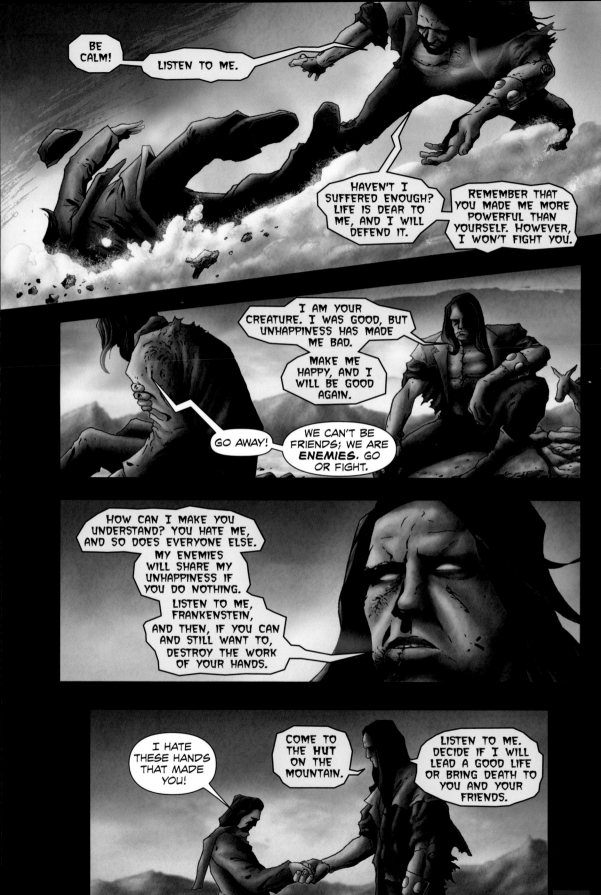

I DECIDED TO LISTEN TO HIS STORY. FOR THE FIRST TIME, I REALIZED THAT AS HIS CREATOR, I HAD DUTIES TOWARD HIM. I FELT I OUGHT TO MAKE HIM HAPPY.

VOLUME II
CHAPTER III

I CAN'T REMEMBER MY FIRST DAYS VERY WELL. I DIDN'T RECOGNIZE MY DIFFERENT SENSES AT FIRST.

I WANTED TO FIND A PLACE THAT HAD **SHADE**, SO I WENT TO THE FOREST NEAR INGOLSTADT.

I ATE SOME FRUIT AND DRANK FROM THE **STREAM**. THEN I LAY DOWN AND WENT TO SLEEP.

IT WAS DARK WHEN I WOKE UP. I FELT COLD AND FRIGHTENED. I HAD TAKEN SOME CLOTHES FROM YOUR APARTMENT, BUT THEY WERE NOT WARM ENOUGH. I SAT AND CRIED.

SOMETIMES I TRIED TO COPY THE SONGS OF THE BIRDS, BUT I COULDN'T. THE NOISES I MADE FRIGHTENED ME INTO SILENCE AGAIN.

SEVERAL DAYS AND NIGHTS PASSED. I SLOWLY BEGAN TO UNDERSTAND WHAT I SAW AND HEARD.

THERE WAS VERY LITTLE FOOD. OFTEN, IT TOOK ME THE WHOLE DAY TO FIND A FEW **NUTS.**

I REALLY WANTED FOOD AND **SHELTER.** EVENTUALLY, I SAW A SMALL **HUT.** THIS WAS A NEW SIGHT TO ME. I EXAMINED IT WITH INTEREST.

THE DOOR WAS OPEN, SO I WENT IN. AN OLD MAN WAS PREPARING HIS BREAKFAST OVER A FIRE.

WHEN HE SAW ME, HE **SCREAMED** AND RAN AWAY.

I WAS SURPRISED, BUT I LIKED THE **HUT** VERY MUCH. SNOW AND RAIN COULD NOT GET IN THERE.

I HUNGRILY ATE THE OLD MAN'S BREAKFAST. THEN I LAY DOWN AND FELL ASLEEP.

IT WAS NOON WHEN I WOKE UP. THE SUN WAS WARM, SO I DECIDED TO TRAVEL FARTHER.

I WALKED FOR SEVERAL HOURS UNTIL I ARRIVED AT A VILLAGE.

AS I ENTERED ONE OF THE COTTAGES, THE CHILDREN INSIDE SCREAMED, AND ONE OF THE WOMEN FAINTED.

SOME OF THE PEOPLE IN THE VILLAGE RAN AWAY, AND OTHERS ATTACKED ME WITH STONES. I RAN AWAY - BACK TO THE FIELDS.

I HID IN A SMALL **HUT**. THERE WAS NOTHING IN IT, BUT IT WAS NEXT TO A PLEASANT **COTTAGE**. I DIDN'T DARE ENTER THE **COTTAGE** AFTER WHAT HAD HAPPENED IN THE VILLAGE.

MY **HUT** WAS MADE OF WOOD AND WAS VERY LOW. I COULD ONLY SIT IN IT WITH DIFFICULTY. THERE WAS NO WOOD ON THE FLOOR, AND THE WIND CAME IN, BUT IT WAS A GOOD **SHELTER**.

I LAY DOWN. I FELT HAPPY TO HAVE A **SHELTER** FROM THE COLD AND FROM THE UNKINDNESS OF HUMANS.

THE NEXT MORNING, I DRANK FROM THE STREAM AND ATE SOME BREAD I HAD STOLEN. I WATCHED THE PEOPLE IN THE **COTTAGE**: A GENTLE YOUNG GIRL, AN UNHAPPY YOUNG MAN, AND AN OLD MAN.

THEY SHOWED SUCH KINDNESS AND LOVE FOR EACH OTHER THAT I BEGAN TO EXPERIENCE NEW FEELINGS.

THEY WERE A MIXTURE OF PAIN AND PLEASURE. I FOUND THEM DIFFICULT TO BEAR.

WHEN NIGHT CAME, THE PEOPLE IN THE **COTTAGE** MADE LIGHT WITH CANDLES. I WAS SURPRISED ...

... AND PLEASED. I COULD CONTINUE WATCHING THEM.

THE NEXT DAY PASSED IN THE SAME WAY. I SOON REALIZED THAT THE OLD MAN WAS BLIND. THE YOUNG PEOPLE SHOWED HIM MUCH LOVE AND RESPECT.

I WANTED VERY MUCH TO JOIN THEM, BUT I DIDN'T DARE. I STAYED IN MY HUT AND TRIED TO UNDERSTAND THEM. THEY WEREN'T HAPPY, ALTHOUGH I COULDN'T SEE A REASON FOR THEIR UNHAPPINESS. I WAS VERY AFFECTED BY IT. WHY WERE SUCH GENTLE CREATURES UNHAPPY?

LATER, I DISCOVERED ONE REASON: THEY WERE POOR.

THEY ATE ONLY VEGETABLES AND DRANK THE MILK OF ONE COW. THEY WERE USUALLY HUNGRY, ESPECIALLY THE YOUNG PEOPLE. OFTEN, THEY GAVE THE OLD MAN FOOD WHEN THEY HAD NONE FOR THEMSELVES.

WHEN I REALIZED THIS, I STOPPED STEALING THEIR FOOD. I ATE ONLY FRUIT AND **NUTS** FROM THE FOREST.

I FOUND ANOTHER WAY I COULD HELP THEM. AT NIGHT, I OFTEN BROUGHT THEM WOOD FOR THEIR FIRE.

AND SLOWLY I DISCOVERED THAT THE WORDS THEY SPOKE PRODUCED PLEASURE OR PAIN, SMILES OR SADNESS. SLOWLY I LEARNED THE NAMES THEY GAVE TO THE MOST FAMILIAR THINGS.

I LEARNED THE WORDS "FIRE," "MILK," "BREAD," AND "WOOD," AND THE NAMES OF THE PEOPLE IN THE **COTTAGE.**

THE OLD MAN WAS "FATHER."

THE GIRL WAS "SISTER" OR "AGATHA."

THE YOUNG MAN WAS "FELIX," "BROTHER," OR "SON."

I WAS VERY HAPPY WHEN I DISCOVERED THE MEANINGS OF THESE SOUNDS AND COULD SAY THEM. I HEARD OTHER WORDS, TOO - "GOOD," "DEAREST," AND "UNHAPPY" - BUT I DIDN'T UNDERSTAND THEM.

I SPENT THE WINTER IN THIS **HUT.**

I BEGAN TO LOVE THE PEOPLE IN THE **COTTAGE.** WHEN THEY WERE UNHAPPY, I FELT SAD. WHEN THEY WERE HAPPY, I WAS HAPPY, TOO.

FELIX WAS ALWAYS THE SADDEST. HE SEEMED TO SUFFER DEEPLY.

BUT HE WAS ABLE TO GIVE PLEASURE TO HIS SISTER. HE GAVE HER THE FIRST LITTLE WHITE FLOWER THAT CAME UP IN THE SNOW.

I ADMIRED THE BEAUTY OF THESE PEOPLE, BUT WHEN I SAW MYSELF IN A POOL OF WATER, I WAS TERRIFIED!

AT FIRST, I COULDN'T BELIEVE WHAT I SAW. THEN I FELT SAD AND ASHAMED. I WAS A **MONSTER.**

EVERY DAY, I DID THE SAME THING: I SLEPT DURING THE DAY AND WENT INTO THE FOREST AT NIGHT.

I COLLECTED MY OWN FOOD AND WOOD FOR THE FAMILY. OFTEN, I CLEARED THEIR PATH OF SNOW. THIS SURPRISED THEM VERY MUCH.

I THOUGHT THAT I COULD MAKE THEM HAPPY. AND I WANTED TO WIN THEIR LOVE. TO DO THIS, I TRIED HARD TO LEARN THEIR LANGUAGE.

63

FELIX?

MY SWEET SAFIE!

SPRING ARRIVED, BUT FELIX WAS STILL VERY SAD. THEN A VISITOR CAME.

FELIX WAS EXTREMELY HAPPY. THE LADY DIDN'T SEEM TO UNDERSTAND HIM BUT SMILED.

THE DAYS PASSED PEACEFULLY. JOY HAD TAKEN THE PLACE OF SADNESS. FELIX BEGAN TO TEACH SAFIE HIS LANGUAGE. I WATCHED THEM CLOSELY SO THAT I COULD LEARN IT, TOO. SAFIE AND I IMPROVED QUICKLY. TWO MONTHS LATER, I COULD UNDERSTAND MOST OF THE WORDS THE FAMILY SAID.

I LISTENED, TOO, AS FELIX TAUGHT SAFIE HISTORY. I LEARNED ABOUT THE MANNERS, GOVERNMENTS, AND RELIGIONS OF DIFFERENT COUNTRIES.

COULD PEOPLE BE SO GOOD, SO
WONDERFUL, SO POWERFUL, AND AT
THE SAME TIME SO **DREADFUL**? WHEN
I HEARD THE TERRIBLE THINGS PEOPLE
HAD DONE, I TURNED AWAY IN **HORROR**.

I THOUGHT ABOUT MYSELF. WHAT WAS I?
I KNEW NOTHING ABOUT MY CREATION
OR MY CREATOR. I WAS EXTREMELY UGLY,
AND I WASN'T THE SAME AS MEN.

VOLUME II CHAPTER VI

THIS FAMILY – WHO WERE THEY?

THE DE LACEYS, FROM PARIS.

THEY CAME FROM A GOOD FRENCH FAMILY. SAFIE'S FATHER HAD RUINED THEM.

HE WAS A TURKISH **MERCHANT** WHO HAD LIVED IN PARIS FOR MANY YEARS. THEN THE GOVERNMENT THREW HIM INTO **PRISON** AND **SENTENCED** HIM TO DEATH.

THERE WAS NO REASON FOR THIS. PEOPLE SAID THE GOVERNMENT DISLIKED HIS RELIGION AND HIS **WEALTH**.

FELIX WAS BY CHANCE AT THIS MAN'S **TRIAL**. FELIX PROMISED TO GET HIM OUT OF **PRISON**.

THE TURK OFFERED HIM MONEY, BUT FELIX REFUSED. THEN HE SAW SAFIE AND WANTED TO MARRY HER.

FELIX TOOK SAFIE AND HER FATHER OUT OF FRANCE. THE **MERCHANT** ENCOURAGED FELIX'S HOPES FOR SAFIE, BUT SECRETLY HE DID NOT WANT HER TO MARRY A **CHRISTIAN**. HE PLANNED TO TAKE HIS DAUGHTER AWAY.

THE MERCHANT'S ESCAPE WAS SOON DISCOVERED, AND FELIX'S FATHER AND SISTER WERE THROWN INTO PRISON.

NEWS OF THIS REACHED FELIX WHO HURRIED BACK TO PARIS.

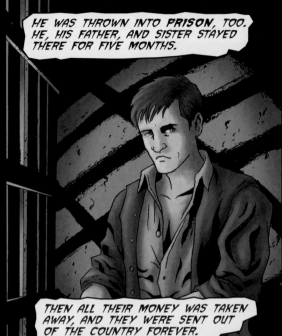

HE WAS THROWN INTO PRISON, TOO. HE, HIS FATHER, AND SISTER STAYED THERE FOR FIVE MONTHS.

THEN ALL THEIR MONEY WAS TAKEN AWAY, AND THEY WERE SENT OUT OF THE COUNTRY FOREVER.

THE MERCHANT HEARD THAT FELIX HAD NO MONEY. HE TOLD HIS DAUGHTER NOT TO THINK OF FELIX ANY MORE.

A FEW DAYS LATER, HE LEFT FOR CONSTANTINOPLE. SAFIE WAS NOW ALONE. IN HER FATHER'S PAPERS, SHE FOUND THE NAME OF FELIX'S NEW HOME IN GERMANY. SHE DECIDED TO GO THERE.

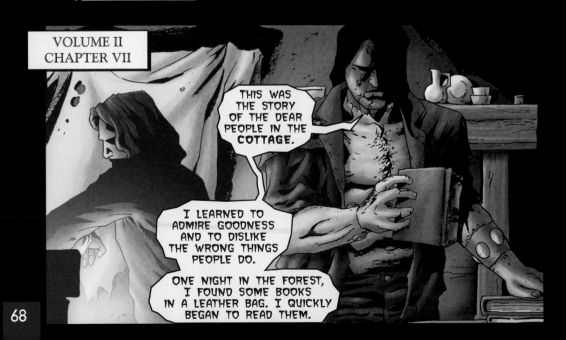

VOLUME II
CHAPTER VII

THIS WAS THE STORY OF THE DEAR PEOPLE IN THE COTTAGE.

I LEARNED TO ADMIRE GOODNESS AND TO DISLIKE THE WRONG THINGS PEOPLE DO.

ONE NIGHT IN THE FOREST, I FOUND SOME BOOKS IN A LEATHER BAG. I QUICKLY BEGAN TO READ THEM.

MY CREATOR HAD LEFT ME, AND IN MY ANGER AND UNHAPPINESS I **CURSED** HIM.

I DECIDED TO INTRODUCE MYSELF TO THE PEOPLE IN THE **COTTAGE** WHEN THE TIME WAS RIGHT. MONTHS PASSED. THEN ONE DAY, WHEN THE OLD MAN WAS ALONE, I KNOCKED ON THE DOOR OF THE **COTTAGE**.

KNOCK KNOCK

WHO'S THERE? COME IN.

PARDON ME. I'M A TRAVELER AND I NEED A LITTLE REST. COULD I SIT FOR A FEW MINUTES BY THE FIRE?

COME IN, BUT I CAN'T OFFER YOU ANY FOOD BECAUSE I'M BLIND.

I HAVE FOOD. I ONLY NEED WARMTH AND REST.

I CANNOT DESCRIBE THEIR *HORROR* WHEN THEY SAW ME.

AGATHA *FAINTED*, AND SAFIE RAN AWAY. FELIX TORE ME FROM HIS FATHER.

MY TRAVELS WERE LONG, AND MY SUFFERINGS WERE **GREAT.** I USUALLY RESTED DURING THE DAY AND TRAVELED AT NIGHT.

HOWEVER, ONE MORNING I FOUND THAT MY PATH WENT THROUGH A DEEP FOREST. I DECIDED TO CONTINUE WALKING AFTER SUNRISE. IT WAS A BEAUTIFUL SPRING DAY, AND I FELT HAPPY.

I HEARD THE SOUND OF VOICES, SO I HID. A YOUNG GIRL RAN ALONG THE **BANK** OF THE RIVER.

SUDDENLY, HER FOOT SLIPPED, AND SHE FELL INTO THE RIVER!

AFTER A FEW WEEKS, MY **WOUND** WAS BETTER, AND I CONTINUED MY JOURNEY. I DIDN'T FIND PLEASURE IN ANYTHING. I JUST FELT EXTREMELY UNHAPPY. AFTER TWO MONTHS, I ARRIVED NEAR GENEVA.

I HID MYSELF IN SOME FIELDS. I WAS TIRED AND HUNGRY. I FELL INTO A LIGHT SLEEP ...

... BUT A BEAUTIFUL CHILD WOKE ME UP.

HE RAN UP TO MY HIDING PLACE. I THOUGHT THAT HE WAS TOO YOUNG TO HATE ME.

AAAHHH!

IF I COULD TEACH HIM TO BE MY FRIEND, I WOULDN'T BE SO LONELY.

FRANKENSTEIN! YOU BELONG TO MY ENEMY!

YOU'LL BE MY FIRST VICTIM!

THE CHILD STILL STRUGGLED AND SHOUTED. I TOOK HOLD OF HIS THROAT TO MAKE HIM STOP ...

... AND IN A MOMENT, HE LAY DEAD AT MY FEET.

I, TOO, CAN CREATE SORROW! THIS DEATH WILL MAKE MY ENEMY MISERABLE AND DESTROY HIM!

I SAW SOMETHING THAT THE CHILD WAS WEARING. IT WAS A PICTURE OF A LOVELY WOMAN.

I REMEMBERED THAT SUCH BEAUTIFUL CREATURES WOULD NEVER BRING ME HAPPINESS.

I WENT TO FIND A HIDING PLACE AND ENTERED A **BARN**. A YOUNG WOMAN WAS SLEEPING THERE. SHE WAS LOVELY.

SHE WAS ONE OF THOSE WHO WOULD NEVER SMILE AT ME.

WAKE UP! YOUR LOVER IS NEAR – SOMEONE WHO WOULD DIE TO HAVE ONE LOOK OF KINDNESS FROM YOU.

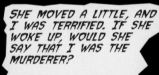

SHE MOVED A LITTLE, AND I WAS TERRIFIED. IF SHE WOKE UP, WOULD SHE SAY THAT I WAS THE MURDERER?

I DECIDED THAT NOT I, BUT SHE, SHOULD SUFFER!

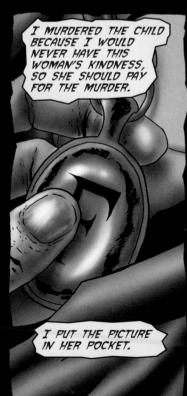

I MURDERED THE CHILD BECAUSE I WOULD NEVER HAVE THIS WOMAN'S KINDNESS, SO SHE SHOULD PAY FOR THE MURDER.

I PUT THE PICTURE IN HER POCKET.

SHE MOVED AGAIN, AND I RAN AWAY.

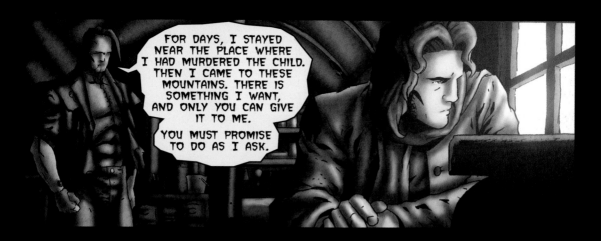

FOR DAYS, I STAYED NEAR THE PLACE WHERE I HAD MURDERED THE CHILD. THEN I CAME TO THESE MOUNTAINS. THERE IS SOMETHING I WANT, AND ONLY YOU CAN GIVE IT TO ME.

YOU MUST PROMISE TO DO AS I ASK.

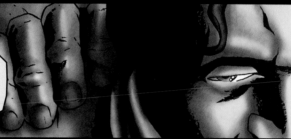

I AM ALONE AND MISERABLE.

PEOPLE HATE ME. YOU MUST CREATE A WOMAN WHO IS AS UGLY AS I AM. SHE WILL NOT RUN AWAY FROM ME. YOU MUST CREATE THIS WOMAN.

VOLUME II
CHAPTER IX

NO!

SHOULD I CREATE ANOTHER CREATURE LIKE YOURSELF WHO WILL HURT PEOPLE? I'LL NEVER AGREE TO IT!

ONLY YOU CAN DO THIS. YOU MUST NOT REFUSE.

I AM DANGEROUS BECAUSE I AM MISERABLE.

WHAT I AM ASKING FOR IS REASONABLE.

DO NOT REFUSE!

ALTHOUGH I FELT AFRAID, I SAW THE TRUTH IN WHAT HE SAID.

HOW CAN YOU LIVE IN WILD PLACES WITHOUT PEOPLE? YOU WANT PEOPLE'S LOVE, AND YOU'LL RETURN TO FIND IT.

I PROMISE YOU THAT I WON'T.

WHY SHOULD I TRUST YOU?

IF YOU AGREE, NEITHER YOU NOR ANYONE ELSE WILL EVER SEE US AGAIN. WE'LL SLEEP ON DRIED LEAVES AND EAT **NUTS** AND FRUIT.

WE'LL LIVE PEACEFULLY.

THEY WILL HATE YOU, AND THEN YOU'LL WANT TO KILL AGAIN.

THE LOVE OF ANOTHER BEING WILL REMOVE THE CAUSE OF MY **CRIMES.**

I'LL DO IT

IF YOU AGREE TO LEAVE EUROPE FOREVER AND NEVER VISIT AN AREA WHERE PEOPLE LIVE.

I PROMISE THAT IF YOU GIVE ME THIS, YOU'LL NEVER SEE ME AGAIN!

GO HOME AND START YOUR WORK. I WILL WATCH YOUR PROGRESS. WHEN YOU'RE READY, I'LL APPEAR!

HE WENT DOWN THE MOUNTAIN EXTREMELY QUICKLY AND DISAPPEARED.

WITH A HEAVY HEART, I WENT DOWN TOWARD THE VALLEY.

I RETURNED TO MY FAMILY IN GENEVA. THEY WERE WORRIED BY MY WILD APPEARANCE. I SAID VERY LITTLE TO THEM, ALTHOUGH I LOVED THEM SO MUCH.

VOLUME III
CHAPTER I

WEEKS PASSED, AND I COULD NOT START MY WORK. I WAS AFRAID OF THE **MONSTER**, BUT I HATED THE TASK TOO MUCH. IT BEGAN TO SEEM LESS NECESSARY TO DO IT.

MY HEALTH WAS MUCH BETTER. WHEN I DIDN'T THINK ABOUT MY PROMISE, I FELT HAPPY.

I'M HAPPY TO SEE YOU BETTER, MY SON, BUT YOU'RE STILL UNHAPPY.

YOU STILL AVOID US. YESTERDAY, I HAD AN IDEA ABOUT WHAT MIGHT BE THE CAUSE OF THIS.

I HAVE ALWAYS **LOOKED FORWARD** TO YOUR MARRIAGE TO ELIZABETH.

BUT PERHAPS YOU THINK OF HER AS A SISTER, OR YOU LOVE SOMEONE ELSE ...

MY DEAR FATHER, I LOVE ELIZABETH AND WANT TO MARRY HER.

IF YOU FEEL THAT WAY, THEN WE WILL CERTAINLY BE HAPPY. TELL ME – WOULD YOU DISLIKE AN IMMEDIATE MARRIAGE?

FOR SOME TIME I COULD NOT REPLY TO MY FATHER.

THE IDEA OF AN IMMEDIATE MARRIAGE FILLED ME WITH **HORROR.**

I HADN'T DONE WHAT I HAD PROMISED THE **MONSTER.** I DIDN'T DARE BREAK MY PROMISE.

FIRST, THE **MONSTER** HAD TO LEAVE WITH HIS **MATE.** THEN I COULD ENJOY THE HAPPINESS OF MARRIAGE IN PEACE.

I REMEMBERED THAT I NEEDED TO GO TO ENGLAND. I HAD TO GET NEW INFORMATION FOR MY TASK.

ALSO, I HAD TO BE AWAY FROM THOSE I LOVED WHILE I WORKED.

I **PERSUADED** MY FATHER TO AGREE TO THE TRIP.

HE HOPED IT WOULD BE GOOD FOR ME.

I COULD GO FOR A FEW MONTHS OR EVEN A YEAR. HE ASKED CLERVAL TO GO WITH ME.

I NEEDED TO BE ALONE TO WORK, BUT IF CLERVAL WAS WITH ME, I WOULDN'T HAVE HOURS FOR LONELY THOUGHT. AND HE MIGHT EVEN STOP THE **MONSTER** FROM VISITING ME.

WE PLANNED THAT ELIZABETH AND I WOULD MARRY WHEN I RETURNED. FOR ME, THIS WAS MY **REWARD** FOR COMPLETING THE TASK I HATED.

I WAS AFRAID OF LEAVING MY FAMILY. MY **ENEMY** COULD ATTACK THEM WHILE I WAS AWAY.

BUT HE HAD PROMISED TO FOLLOW ME EVERYWHERE, SO WOULD HE NOT COME TO ENGLAND?

WE DECIDED TO STAY IN LONDON FOR A FEW MONTHS.

IT WAS A WONDERFUL CITY, BUT I COULDN'T ENJOY IT.

A DARK CLOUD HUNG OVER ME.

THIS IS LIVING!

CLERVAL WANTED TO MEET MEN WHO WERE CLEVER AND FULL OF NEW IDEAS. THIS WAS NOT IMPORTANT TO ME.

MY AIM WAS TO GET THE INFORMATION I NEEDED FOR MY TASK.

I TOOK MY LETTERS OF INTRODUCTION TO THE MOST FAMOUS NATURAL SCIENTISTS.

I VISITED THESE PEOPLE ONLY FOR THE INFORMATION THEY COULD GIVE ME.

I FELT *DESPAIR* WHEN I WAS WITH OTHER PEOPLE. I WASN'T LIKE THEM.

CLERVAL WAS HOW I HAD BEEN IN THE PAST: HE WANTED TO LEARN AND DO NEW THINGS. HE WAS ALSO WORKING TOWARD ACHIEVING SOMETHING HE HAD WANTED FOR A LONG TIME.

HE WANTED TO GO TO INDIA SO THAT HE COULD BECOME A TRADER THERE.

HE WAS ALWAYS BUSY. I OFTEN REFUSED TO GO PLACES WITH HIM SO THAT I COULD BE ALONE.

I BEGAN TO COLLECT THE MATERIALS THAT I NEEDED FOR MY NEW CREATION.

I HATED DOING IT.

AFTER A FEW MONTHS IN LONDON, WE RECEIVED AN INVITATION FROM A FRIEND IN THE NORTH OF SCOTLAND. I DIDN'T LIKE BEING WITH PEOPLE, BUT I WANTED VERY MUCH TO SEE MOUNTAINS AND **STREAMS** AGAIN. WE ACCEPTED THE INVITATION.

ON THE WAY TO EDINBURGH, WE VISITED WINDSOR, OXFORD, MATLOCK, AND THE CUMBERLAND LAKES.

I TOOK MY EQUIPMENT AND MATERIALS SO THAT I COULD FINISH MY WORK IN THE NORTH OF SCOTLAND.

HENRY LOVED THE BEAUTY OF EDINBURGH, BUT I WANTED TO FINISH THE JOURNEY.

SOMETIMES I THOUGHT THE **MONSTER** HAD FOLLOWED ME. I WAS AFRAID HE WOULD KILL HENRY BECAUSE I WASN'T WORKING FAST ENOUGH.

I WANTED TO FIND A PLACE THAT WAS VERY FAR FROM EVERYTHING. I CHOSE A SMALL, ROCKY ISLAND IN THE ORKNEYS. ONLY FIVE PEOPLE AND A FEW COWS LIVED THERE.

I LIVED IN A SMALL **HUT**. I WORKED DURING THE DAY, AND IN THE EVENING I WALKED ALONG THE STONY BEACH TO LISTEN TO THE **WAVES** AS THEY CRASHED AT MY FEET.

AS THE DAYS PASSED, I BEGAN TO HATE MY WORK MORE AND MORE. SOMETIMES I COULDN'T DO IT AT ALL ...

... AND AT OTHER TIMES, I WORKED DAY AND NIGHT. I BECAME RESTLESS AND NERVOUS. THE WHOLE TIME I WAS AFRAID OF MEETING THE **MONSTER**.

WHEN I WORKED ON MY FIRST EXPERIMENT, I FELT EXCITED. THIS TIME, I FELT SICK.

VOLUME III
CHAPTER III

ONE EVENING, I BEGAN TO THINK ABOUT WHAT I WAS DOING.

THREE YEARS EARLIER, I HAD CREATED A **MONSTER** WHO HAD DONE **DREADFUL** THINGS.

NOW I WAS MAKING ANOTHER CREATURE. I DIDN'T KNOW WHAT SHE WOULD DO.

PERHAPS SHE WOULD BE WORSE THAN HER **MATE** AND KILL FOR PLEASURE.
CRACK!
BOOM!
HE HAD PROMISED TO LIVE FAR AWAY FROM EVERYONE, BUT SHE HAD NOT MADE THAT PROMISE.
PERHAPS SHE WOULD REFUSE TO.

PERHAPS THEY WOULD HATE EACH OTHER. HE MIGHT THINK SHE WAS UGLY.

SHE MIGHT TURN AWAY FROM HIM. SHE MIGHT LEAVE HIM AND MAKE HIM MORE **MISERABLE**.

OR THEY COULD HAVE CHILDREN WHO MIGHT BE DANGEROUS.

FOR THE FIRST TIME, I REALIZED WHAT I HAD DONE. I HAD BOUGHT MY OWN PEACE AT THE PRICE, PERHAPS, OF THE EXISTENCE OF THE WHOLE **HUMAN RACE**.

SUDDENLY...

!?!

94

... YES, HE HAD FOLLOWED ME. NOW HE HAD COME TO CLAIM WHAT I HAD PROMISED HIM.

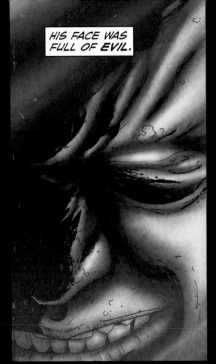
HIS FACE WAS FULL OF *EVIL*.

I FELT CRAZY WHEN I THOUGHT OF MY PROMISE TO CREATE ANOTHER *MONSTER* LIKE HIM.

AAAARRRGGGHHH!!

THUNK!!

SQUELCH!!

THUDD!!

THE **MONSTER** WATCHED IN **HORROR** AS I DESTROYED THE ONLY CREATURE THAT COULD BRING HIM HAPPINESS.

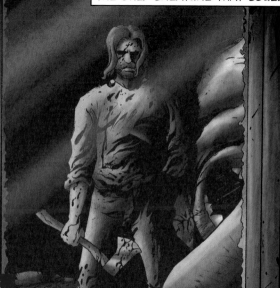

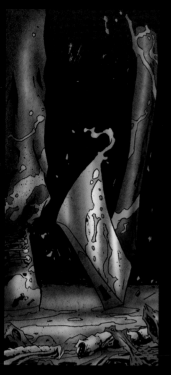

HE GAVE A CRY OF **DESPAIR** AND **REVENGE** AND DISAPPEARED.

I PROMISED MYSELF THAT I WOULD NEVER WORK ON THIS TASK AGAIN.

SEVERAL HOURS PASSED; THEN I HEARD THE SOUND OF A BOAT. SOMEBODY LANDED NEAR MY HOUSE.

YOU HAVE DESTROYED YOUR WORK! DO YOU INTEND TO BREAK YOUR PROMISE TO ME? DO YOU DARE DESTROY MY HOPES?

YES, I WILL BREAK MY PROMISE. I WILL NEVER CREATE ANOTHER CREATURE LIKE YOU AGAIN!

REMEMBER THAT I HAVE POWER.

YOU ARE MY CREATOR, BUT I AM YOUR MASTER. OBEY!

BEFORE YOU KILL ME, BE SURE OF YOUR OWN SAFETY!

HE DISAPPEARED IN HIS BOAT, AND EVERYTHING WAS SILENT AGAIN.

I THOUGHT AGAIN OF HIS WORDS ...

"I WILL BE WITH YOU ON YOUR **WEDDING** NIGHT".

THAT WAS GOING TO BE THE DAY OF MY DEATH. I DID NOT FEEL AFRAID. I FELT SORRY FOR ELIZABETH. I DECIDED NOT TO DIE WITHOUT A FIGHT.

THE NEXT DAY, I RECEIVED A LETTER FROM CLERVAL. HE ASKED ME TO JOIN HIM AGAIN. THE LETTER BROUGHT ME BACK TO REAL LIFE, AND I DECIDED TO LEAVE THE ISLAND.

I PACKED UP MY EQUIPMENT AND THE PARTS OF THE UNFINISHED CREATURE. VERY EARLY THE NEXT MORNING, I SAILED OUT AND THREW THEM INTO THE SEA.

THE AIR WAS SO PURE THAT I DECIDED TO STAY LONGER ON THE WATER. EVENTUALLY, CLOUDS HID THE MOON. EVERYTHING WAS DARK, AND I HEARD ONLY THE SOUND OF THE BOAT. IN A SHORT TIME, I FELL ASLEEP.

WHEN I WOKE UP, THE SUN WAS QUITE HIGH IN THE SKY. THE WIND WAS HIGH, TOO, AND THE **WAVES** WERE THREATENING THE SAFETY OF MY BOAT.

THE WIND HAD DRIVEN ME A LONG WAY FROM THE COAST.

WHEN I TRIED TO CHANGE DIRECTION, WATER QUICKLY FILLED THE BOAT. I COULD ONLY SAIL WITH THE WIND BEHIND ME.

I LOOKED AT THE SEA. IT WAS GOING TO BE MY **GRAVE**.

MONSTER! YOU'VE GOT WHAT YOU WANTED!

SOME HOURS PASSED IN THIS WAY ...

... BUT SLOWLY THE WIND BECAME GENTLER, AND THE SEA BECAME CALMER. I WAS FEELING SICK AND VERY TIRED WHEN SUDDENLY I SAW LAND.

I CRIED WITH JOY. I KNEW I WAS FINALLY SAFE.

MY GOOD FRIENDS -

- WILL YOU TELL ME THE NAME OF THIS TOWN? WHERE AM I?

YOU'LL KNOW SOON.

YOU MIGHT NOT LIKE THE PLACE, BUT YOU WON'T BE ABLE TO CHOOSE WHERE YOU STAY.

WHY DO YOU ANSWER ME SO ROUGHLY?

SURELY THE ENGLISH DO NOT USUALLY SPEAK TO STRANGERS SO UNKINDLY.

I DON'T KNOW WHAT THE ENGLISH DO, BUT THE IRISH HATE **EVIL** PEOPLE.

YOU MUST COME WITH ME TO MR. KIRWIN, THE JUDGE.

YOU MUST TELL HIM ABOUT THE MURDER OF A MAN HERE LAST NIGHT.

I WAS TAKEN TO THE JUDGE, AN OLD MAN WITH CALM AND KIND MANNERS. HE LOOKED AT ME, HOWEVER, QUITE UNKINDLY.

WHO IS APPEARING AS A **WITNESS**?

I AM, SIR.

I WAS OUT IN MY BOAT WITH MY **BROTHER-IN-LAW** DANIEL NUGENT.

AS I WAS WALKING HOME ALONG THE BEACH, I HIT MY FOOT ON THE BODY OF A MAN. HIS CLOTHES WERE DRY. SOMEONE HAD KILLED HIM.

THE BLACK MARKS FROM THE **MONSTER'S** FINGERS WERE ON HIS NECK.

I REMEMBERED MY BROTHER'S MURDER, AND I FELT EXTREMELY SHAKEN.

MR. KIRWIN SAW THAT I WAS BADLY AFFECTED. OF COURSE HE THOUGHT I WAS **GUILTY**.

MY NAME IS DANIEL NUGENT, SIR.

JUST BEFORE WE FOUND THE BODY, I SAW A MAN IN A BOAT QUITE CLOSE TO THE **SHORE**.

IT LOOKED LIKE THE SAME BOAT THAT THIS MAN HAS JUST LANDED IN.

A WOMAN ALSO SAW A MAN IN A BOAT. HE SAILED AWAY FROM THE PLACE WHERE THE BODY WAS FOUND.

THEY ALL AGREED THAT THE STRONG WIND HAD DRIVEN ME BACK TO THE **SHORE** – TO WHERE I HAD LEFT THE BODY.

SHOW HIM THE BODY.

I WANT TO SEE HOW HE REACTS.

I WAS CALM.

I KNEW THAT THE PEOPLE ON THE ISLAND I HAD LEFT COULD **PROVE** MY **INNOCENCE**. I WAS TALKING TO THEM WHEN THE BODY WAS FOUND.

NO!! MY DEAREST HENRY!! NOT YOU, TOO!!!

I HAVE ALREADY DESTROYED TWO PEOPLE ...

... BUT YOU, CLERVAL, MY FRIEND ...

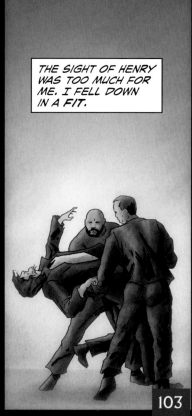

THE SIGHT OF HENRY WAS TOO MUCH FOR ME. I FELL DOWN IN A **FIT**.

I WAS VERY SICK FOR TWO MONTHS. I SAID SOME **DREADFUL** THINGS IN MY ILLNESS, I LEARNED LATER.

I CALLED MYSELF THE MURDERER OF WILLIAM, JUSTINE, AND CLERVAL.

FORTUNATELY, ONLY MR. KIRWIN UNDERSTOOD MY NATIVE LANGUAGE, BUT MY LOUD CRIES FRIGHTENED THE OTHER PEOPLE AROUND ME.

WHY DIDN'T I DIE? I WAS MORE **MISERABLE** THAN ANYONE HAD EVER BEEN BEFORE.

BUT I SURVIVED, AND AFTER TWO MONTHS I WOKE UP IN **PRISON.**

ARE YOU BETTER NOW, SIR?

I BELIEVE I AM.

I'M SORRY I'M STILL ALIVE TO FEEL THIS PAIN AND **HORROR.**

YES, IT WOULD BE BETTER FOR YOU IF YOU WERE **DEAD**. BUT THAT'S NONE OF MY BUSINESS.

I AM JUST HERE TO TAKE CARE OF YOU AND TO MAKE YOU WELL.

I SOON LEARNED THAT MR. KIRWIN HAD BEEN EXTREMELY KIND TO ME. HE HAD GIVEN ME THE BEST ROOM IN THE **PRISON** AND A DOCTOR AND A NURSE.

ONE DAY, WHILE I WAS SLOWLY **RECOVERING,** HE VISITED ME.

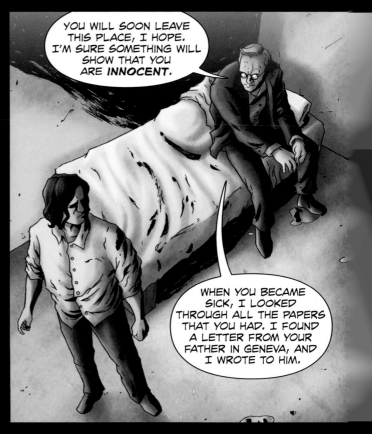

YOU WILL SOON LEAVE THIS PLACE, I HOPE. I'M SURE SOMETHING WILL SHOW THAT YOU ARE **INNOCENT**.

WHEN YOU BECAME SICK, I LOOKED THROUGH ALL THE PAPERS THAT YOU HAD. I FOUND A LETTER FROM YOUR FATHER IN GENEVA, AND I WROTE TO HIM.

OH NO!! TELL ME –

– WHO IS **DEAD** NOW?

YOUR FAMILY IS PERFECTLY WELL ...

... AND SOMEONE HAS COME TO VISIT YOU.

FATHER! YOU'RE SAFE!

AND ELIZABETH?

AND ERNEST?

EVERYONE IS SAFE. WHAT A PLACE THIS IS, MY SON!

YOU TRAVELED TO FIND HAPPINESS, BUT SOMETHING TERRIBLE SEEMS TO FOLLOW YOU.

AND POOR CLERVAL!

I HAD TO TRAVEL NEARLY A HUNDRED MILES TO APPEAR IN COURT. MR. KIRWIN ARRANGED MY DEFENSE.

THE COURT DECIDED THAT I WAS **INNOCENT**. WE **PROVED** THAT I WAS ON THE ORKNEY ISLANDS WHEN THE BODY WAS FOUND.

I WAS ALLOWED TO GO FREE. I COULD BREATHE FRESH AIR AND GO HOME. BUT FOR ME, EVERYWHERE WAS HATEFUL. I OFTEN WANTED TO END MY LIFE, BUT I STILL HAD ONE DUTY. I HAD TO TAKE CARE OF THE PEOPLE I LOVED. AND I HAD TO FIGHT THE MURDERER.

VOLUME III
CHAPTER V

WHEN WE REACHED PARIS, I RECEIVED A LETTER FROM ELIZABETH.

... TELL ME, DEAREST VICTOR - DO YOU LOVE SOMEONE ELSE?

I LOVE YOU, BUT IT IS YOUR HAPPINESS THAT I DESIRE.

ELIZABETH

I REMEMBERED THE **MONSTER'S** THREAT: "I WILL BE WITH YOU ON YOUR **WEDDING** NIGHT!"

HE HAD DECIDED TO KILL ME ON THAT NIGHT. SWEET ELIZABETH! I WOULD DIE TO MAKE HER HAPPY.

MY DEAREST ELIZABETH, I AM AFRAID THAT LITTLE HAPPINESS REMAINS FOR US ON EARTH. HOWEVER, ALL MY FUTURE HAPPINESS IS CENTERED ON YOU. I PROMISE MYSELF TO YOU AND NO ONE ELSE.

I HAVE ONE, **DREADFUL** SECRET WHICH WILL FILL YOU WITH **HORROR.** I WILL TELL IT TO YOU THE DAY AFTER OUR MARRIAGE. UNTIL THEN, DO NOT MENTION IT.

VICTOR

WE RETURNED TO GENEVA. ELIZABETH WELCOMED ME WARMLY.

HAVE YOU PROMISED YOURSELF TO ANOTHER WOMAN?

NO. I LOVE ELIZABETH AND AM **LOOKING FORWARD** TO OUR WEDDING.

LET'S FIX THE DATE NOW.

WE GOT MARRIED TEN DAYS LATER. I CARRIED A KNIFE AND A **GUN** TO PROTECT MYSELF. ELIZABETH SEEMED HAPPY, AND MY FATHER WAS FULL OF JOY.

BUT I HAD ONLY PREPARED FOR MY OWN DEATH, NOT FOR THE DEATH OF ANYONE DEAR TO ME.

ELIZABETH HAD *INHERITED* FROM HER FAMILY A SMALL HOUSE BY LAKE COMO. WE PLANNED TO SPEND OUR FIRST DAYS THERE. AFTER THE *WEDDING*, WE WENT BY BOAT TO EVIAN.

YOU'RE SAD, MY LOVE.

LET ME ENJOY THE HAPPINESS OF TODAY AFTER EVERYTHING I HAVE SUFFERED.

BE HAPPY, MY DEAR VICTOR.

SOMETHING WHISPERS TO ME THAT I MUSTN'T *LOOK FORWARD* TO HAPPINESS, BUT I WON'T LISTEN TO SUCH A VOICE.

WHAT A BEAUTIFUL DAY! HOW HAPPY AND CALM NATURE LOOKS.

THOSE WERE THE LAST MOMENTS OF MY LIFE WHEN I FELT HAPPY.

AS WE REACHED THE *SHORE*, MY FEAR RETURNED. IT HAS STAYED WITH ME AND WILL STAY FOREVER.

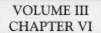

WE TOOK A SHORT WALK ALONG THE **SHORE** AND ADMIRED THE LOVELY SCENE.

SUDDENLY, THE WIND GREW STRONGER, AND A HEAVY RAIN CAME DOWN. I WAS ANXIOUS AND HELD TIGHTLY TO MY **GUN.**

WHAT ARE YOU AFRAID OF, VICTOR?

OH! IT'S JUST THE STORM.

IT'S A **DREADFUL** NIGHT.

PLEASE GO TO BED, MY LOVE. I'LL JOIN YOU LATER.

VICTOR ...

SHE LEFT ME, AND I SEARCHED THE HOUSE FOR THE **MONSTER** ...

... BUT I FOUND NOTHING.

AAAAHH!!!

SHRIEK!!

AS I HEARD THE **SCREAM**, I REALIZED WHAT WAS HAPPENING!

ELIZABETH!!!

I FAINTED.

WHEN I *RECOVERED*, I RUSHED TOWARD HER. I HELD HER IN MY ARMS.

THE *MARKS* OF THE *MONSTER'S* FINGERS WERE ON HER NECK.

I LOOKED UP AT THE WINDOW ...

... AND SAW THE *MONSTER*. HE SEEMED TO SMILE AS HE POINTED TO THE *DEAD* BODY OF MY WIFE.

BANG!

BANG!

HE RAN AWAY AND INTO THE LAKE.

THE SOUND OF THE **GUN** ATTRACTED A CROWD WHO HELPED ME LOOK FOR THE **MONSTER**. AFTER SEVERAL HOURS, WE RETURNED. WE HADN'T FOUND HIM. MANY OF THE PEOPLE THOUGHT THAT I HAD IMAGINED HIM.

I WAS IN A CLOUD OF CONFUSION AND **HORROR**.

THE DEATHS OF WILLIAM, JUSTINE, CLERVAL, AND NOW MY WIFE ...

... MY FATHER AND ERNEST MIGHT DIE NEXT!

I DECIDED TO RETURN TO GENEVA AS QUICKLY AS POSSIBLE.

WHEN I WAS ALLOWED TO LEAVE, I VISITED A JUDGE IN THE TOWN. I WANTED TO TELL HIM ABOUT THE *MONSTER*.

SIR, I KNOW WHO MURDERED MY BROTHER AND MY WIFE.

I WANT YOU TO HELP ME FIND HIM.

I'LL DO EVERYTHING THAT I CAN, SIR.

THANK YOU. MY STORY'S STRANGE, BUT IT'S ALL TRUE.

I TOLD HIM MY STORY. AT FIRST HE COULDN'T BELIEVE IT. BUT AS I CONTINUED, HE BECAME MORE INTERESTED.

IT'S YOUR DUTY TO CATCH THIS MURDERER.

I'D LIKE TO, BUT THIS CREATURE SOUNDS TOO POWERFUL.

AND NO ONE KNOWS WHERE HE COULD BE NOW.

YOU REFUSE TO HELP ME!

THEN I'LL FIND HIM MYSELF! I'LL DESTROY HIM!

I LEFT HIS HOUSE ANGRILY. I WENT AWAY TO THINK ABOUT WHAT TO DO.

VOLUME III
CHAPTER VII

REVENGE GAVE ME STRENGTH. I DECIDED TO LEAVE GENEVA FOREVER.

BUT FIRST, I FOUND MYSELF BY THE **GRAVES** OF WILLIAM, ELIZABETH, AND MY FATHER.

THEIR **SPIRITS** SEEMED TO FLY AROUND. I FELT VERY ANGRY.

I WILL FOLLOW THE **MONSTER** WHO HAS CAUSED THESE DEATHS UNTIL EITHER HE DIES OR I DIE!

LET HIM FEEL THE **DREADFUL** SADNESS THAT I FEEL!

HA HA HA HA HA! I'M HAPPY.

YOU'VE DECIDED TO LIVE, **MISERABLE** CREATURE!

I RAN TOWARD HIM, BUT HE ESCAPED.

I RAN AFTER HIM AND HAVE BEEN FOLLOWING HIM FOR MANY MONTHS.

LETTER - AUGUST 26, 17--

MY DEAR MARGARET, YOU HAVE READ THIS STRANGE AND TERRIBLE STORY. I BELIEVE THAT IT IS TRUE. THIS **MONSTER** REALLY EXISTS! SOMETIMES I ASKED FRANKENSTEIN ABOUT HOW HE MADE THIS CREATURE ...

ARE YOU CRAZY, MY FRIEND? DO YOU WANT TO CREATE ANOTHER **MONSTER**?

LEARN FROM MY MISTAKES AND DON'T MAKE YOURSELF COMPLETELY **MISERABLE.**

I HAVE FINALLY FOUND THE FRIEND I WAS LOOKING FOR. HOWEVER, I THINK I WILL LOSE HIM. HE HAS NO INTEREST IN LIFE AT ALL.

THANK YOU FOR YOUR KINDNESS, WALTON, BUT ALL MY FRIENDS ARE **DEAD.** NO ONE CAN REPLACE THEM.

ONLY ONE THOUGHT KEEPS ME ALIVE. I MUST FOLLOW AND DESTROY THE **MONSTER** I CREATED.

THEN I CAN DIE.

LETTER - SEPTEMBER 2, 17--

MY DEAREST SISTER,

WE ARE **SURROUNDED** BY MOUNTAINS OF ICE. THE **BRAVE** MEN WHO ARE WITH ME ARE IN DANGER. THEY LOOK TO ME FOR HELP, BUT I CAN'T GIVE THEM ANY. MY CRAZY SCHEMES MAY BE THE CAUSE OF OUR DEATHS.

LETTER –
SEPTEMBER 5, 17--

I WAS AFRAID THAT THE MEN WOULD REFUSE TO OBEY ME.

CAPTAIN, IF THE SHIP GETS FREE OF THE ICE, YOU MUST TAKE US SOUTH.

WE INSIST.

WHAT DO YOU MEAN?

WHAT ARE YOU DEMANDING?

ARE YOU RUNNING AWAY AT THE FIRST SIGN OF DANGER? GO HOME AS MEN WHO HAVE SUCCEEDED, NOT FAILED.

THE MEN WERE UNABLE TO REPLY.

THINK ABOUT IT.

I WILL NOT LEAD YOU FARTHER NORTH IF YOU DO NOT WANT TO GO.

YES, CAPTAIN.

LETTER - SEPTEMBER 7, 17--

THE MATTER IS SETTLED. I HAVE AGREED TO RETURN IF WE GET FREE OF THE ICE. I AM VERY DISAPPOINTED.

September 12, 17--

It is over. I am returning to England. I have lost my hopes of glory - and I have lost my friend.

Three days ago, the ice began to move. Islands of ice broke off in all directions. We were in great danger, but we could do nothing. My unfortunate guest was so sick that he had to stay in bed.

HURRAH!

YEAH!

HOORAY!

THEY'RE HAPPY BECAUSE THIS MEANS WE'LL SOON GO BACK TO ENGLAND.

ARE YOU REALLY GOING TO GO BACK?

YES. I CAN'T LEAD THEM INTO **GREATER** DANGER.

121

HE SQUEEZED MY HAND WEAKLY AND CLOSED HIS EYES FOREVER.

MARGARET, WHAT CAN I SAY ABOUT THE DEATH OF THIS WONDERFUL MAN? HOW CAN I EXPRESS THE DEPTH OF MY **SORROW**?

THUD!

THAT NOISE ...

... A VOICE ...

... FROM FRANKENSTEIN'S ROOM!

GREAT GOD!

WHEN HE HEARD ME, HE RAN TOWARD THE WINDOW.

STAY!

I DON'T WANT YOU TO FEEL SORRY FOR ME. I'M CONTENT TO SUFFER ALONE.

AT ONE TIME, I HOPED FOR HUMAN LOVE, BUT MY **CRIMES** HAVE PLACED ME BELOW THE LOWEST ANIMAL.

WHEN I REMEMBER EVERYTHING THAT I HAVE DONE, I CANNOT BELIEVE THAT I AM THE SAME CREATURE THAT AT ONE TIME WANTED ONLY BEAUTY AND GOODNESS.

BUT IT IS SO: THE FALLEN **ANGEL** BECOMES A **DEVIL.**

SOON, I WILL DIE, AND MY UNHAPPINESS WILL BE OVER. I WILL BE HAPPY AT LAST IN THE PAIN OF THE FIRE!

AAARRRRGGGHHH!!!

MY SPIRIT WILL SLEEP IN PEACE.

Frankenstein

End

Glossary

A

adopt /ədɒpt/ – (adopts, adopting, adopted) If you adopt someone else's child, you take it into your own family and make it legally your son or daughter.

Alpine /ælpaɪn/ – Apline means existing in or relating to mountains.

angel /eɪndʒəl/ – (angels) Angels are spiritual beings that some people believe are God's servants in heaven.

arrest /ərɛst/ – (arrests, arresting, arrested) If the police arrest you, they take charge of you and take you to a police station because they believe you may have committed a crime.

astonishing /əstɒnɪʃɪŋ/ – Something that is astonishing is very surprising.

B

bank /bæŋk/ – (banks) The banks of a river, canal, or lake are the raised areas of ground along its edge.

barn /barn/ – (barns) A barn is a building on a farm in which animals, animal food, or crops can be kept.

bear /bɛər/ – (bears, bearing, bore, borne) If you bear an unpleasant experience, you accept it because you are unable to do anything about it.

beat /bit/ – (beats, beating, beat, beaten) When your heart or pulse beats, it continually makes regular rhythmic movements.

blame /bleɪm/ – (blames, blaming, blamed) If you blame a person or thing for something bad or if you blame something bad on somebody, you believe or say that they are responsible for it or that they caused it.

board /bɔrd/ – (boards, boarding, boarded) When you board a train, ship, or aircraft, you get on it in order to travel somewhere.

brave /breɪv/ – Someone who is brave is willing to do things that are dangerous and does not show fear in difficult or dangerous situations.

brother-in-law /brʌðər ɪn lɔ/ – (brothers-in-law) Someone's brother-in-law is the brother of their husband or wife, or the man who is married to their sister.

C

captain /kæptɪn/ – (captains) In the army, navy, and some other armed forces, a captain is an officer of middle rank.

Christian /krɪstʃən/ – (Christians) A Christian is someone who follows the teachings of Jesus Christ.

confess /kənfɛs/ – (confesses, confessing, confessed) If you confess to doing something wrong or something that you are ashamed of, you admit that you did it.

cottage /kɒtɪdʒ/ – (cottages) A cottage is a small house, usually in the country.

courtyard /kɔrtyard/ – (courtyards) A courtyard is an open area of ground which is surrounded by buildings or walls.

crime /kraɪm/ – (crimes) A crime is an illegal action or activity for which a person can be punished by law.

cross /krɔs/ – (crosses, crossing, crossed) If you cross a room, road, or area of land, you move to the other side of it. If you cross to a place, you move over or travel over a room, road, or area in order to reach that place.

curse /kɜrs/ – (curses, cursing, cursed) If you curse someone or something, you say impolite or insulting things about them because you are angry with them.

D

dead /dɛd/ – A person, animal, or plant that is dead is no longer living.

decay /dɪkeɪ/ – (decays, decaying, decayed) When something such as a dead body, a dead plant, or a tooth decays, it is gradually destroyed by a natural process.

deserve /dɪzɜrv/ – (deserves, deserving, deserved) If you say that a person or thing deserves something, you mean that they should have or receive it because of their actions or qualities.

despair /dɪspɛər/ – Despair is the feeling that everything is wrong and that nothing will improve.

destiny /dɛstɪni/ – (destinies) A person's destiny is everything that happens to them during their life, including what will happen in the future, especially when it is considered to be controlled by someone or something else. Destiny is the force which some people believe controls the things that happen to you in your life.

devil /dɛvəl/ – (devils) In Judaism, Christianity, and Islam, the Devil is the most powerful evil spirit. A devil is an evil spirit.

disease /dɪziz/ – (diseases) A disease is an illness which affects people, animals, or plants.

disgusting /dɪsgʌstɪŋ/ – If you say that something is disgusting, you think it is extremely unpleasant or unacceptable.

dreadful /drɛdfəl/ – If you say that something is dreadful, you mean that it is very unpleasant or very poor in quality.

dull /dʌl/ – (duller, dullest) A dull color or light is not bright.

E

embrace /ɪmbreɪs/ – (embraces, embracing, embraced) If you embrace someone, you put your arms around them in order to show affection for them. You can also say that two people embrace.

enemy /ɛnəmi/ – (enemies) If someone is your enemy, they hate you or want to harm you. The enemy is an army or other force that is opposed to you in a war, or a country with which your country is at war.

evil /ivəl/ – (evils) Evil is used to refer to all the wicked and bad things that happen in the world. An evil is a very unpleasant or harmful situation or activity. If you describe someone or something as evil, you mean that you think they are morally very bad and cause harm to people.

F

faint /feɪnt/ – (faints, fainting, fainted) If you faint, you lose consciousness for a short time.

fit /fɪt/ – (fits) If someone has a fit, they suddenly lose consciousness and their body makes uncontrollable movements.

flash /flæʃ/ – (flashes) A flash is a sudden burst of light or of something shiny or bright.

forgive /fərgɪv/ – (forgives, forgiving, forgave, forgiven) If you forgive someone who has done something bad or wrong, you stop being angry with them and no longer want to punish them.

frozen /frouzən/ – If the ground is frozen, it has become very hard because the weather is very cold. If you say that you are frozen or a part of your body is frozen, you are emphasizing that you feel very cold.

funeral /fyunərəl/ – (funerals) A funeral is the ceremony that is held when the body of someone who has died is buried or cremated.

G

glory /glɔri/ – (glories) Glory is fame and admiration that you gain by doing something impressive.

grave /greɪv/ – (graves) A grave is a hole in which a dead person is buried.

graveyard /greɪvyard/ – (graveyards) A graveyard is an area of land where dead people are buried.

great /greɪt/ – (greater, greatest) Great means large in amount or degree.

guilt /gɪlt/ – Guilt is an unhappy feeling that you have because you have done something wrong or think that you have done something wrong. Guilt is the fact that you have done something wrong or illegal.

guilty /gɪlti/ – (guiltier, guiltiest) If someone is guilty of doing something wrong or committing a crime or offense, they have done that thing or committed that crime.

gun /gʌn/ – (guns) A gun is a weapon from which bullets or other things are fired.

H

heaven /hɛvən/ – (heavens) In some religions, heaven is said to be the place where God lives and where good people go when they die.

hell /hɛl/ – In some religions, hell is the place where the Devil lives and where bad people are sent when they die. If you say that a particular situation or place is hell, you are emphasizing that it is extremely unpleasant.

horror /hɔrər/ – (horrors) Horror is a feeling of great shock, fear, and worry caused by something extremely unpleasant.

hut /hʌt/ – (huts) A hut is a small, simple building, especially one made of wood, mud, grass, or stones.

I

inherit /ɪnhɛrɪt/ – (inherits, inheriting, inherited) If you inherit money or property, you receive it from someone who has died.

innocence /ɪnəsəns/ – If someone proves their innocence, they prove that they are not guilty of a crime.

innocent /ɪnəsənt/ – If someone is innocent, they did not commit a crime that they have been accused of.

L

lecture /lɛktʃər/ – (lectures) A lecture is a talk someone gives in order to teach people about a particular subject, usually at a university or college.

lightning /laɪtnɪŋ/ – Lightning is the very bright flashes of light in the sky that happen during thunderstorms.

long /lɔŋ/ – (longs, longing, longed) If you long for something, you want it very much.

look forward to /lʊk fɔrwərd tə/ – If you look forward to something that is going to happen, you want it to happen because you think you will enjoy it.

M

mark /mark/ – (marks) A mark is a small area of something such as dirt that has accidentally gotten onto a surface or piece of clothing.

master /mæstər/ – (masters) A servant's master is the man that he or she works for. If you say that someone is a master of a particular activity, you mean that they are extremely skilled at it.

mate /meɪt/ – (mates) An animal's mate is its sexual partner.

merchant /mɜrtʃənt/ – (merchants) A merchant is a person who buys or sells goods in large quantities.

miserable /mɪzərəbəl/ – If you are miserable, you are very unhappy.

Monsieur /məsyɜr/ – (Messieurs) Monsieur is the French title of respect and term of address for a man, similar to "Mister."

monster /mɒnstər/ – (monsters) A monster is a large imaginary creature that looks very ugly and frightening.

N

nobleman /noʊbəlmæn/ – (noblemen) In former times, a nobleman was a man who was a member of the nobility.

nonsense /nɒnsɛns/ – If you say that something spoken or written is nonsense, you think that it is untrue or silly.

nut /nʌt/ – (nuts) The firm shelled fruit of some trees and bushes are called nuts.

P

pale /peɪl/ – (paler, palest) Something that is pale is not strong or bright in color.

Paradise Lost – Poem written by the English poet John Milton in 1667, about the fall of Man (the expulsion of Adam and Eve from the Garden of Eden after falling into the temptation of Satan)

persuade /pərsweɪd/ – (persuades, persuading, persuaded) If you persuade someone to do something, you cause them to do it by giving them good reasons for doing it.

poet /poʊɪt/ – (poets) A poet is a person who writes poems.

prison /prɪzən/ – (prisons) A prison is a building where criminals are kept as punishment.

professor /prəfɛsər/ – (professors) A professor in an American or Canadian university or college is a teacher of the highest rank. A professor in a British university is the most senior teacher in a department.

prove /pruv/ – (proves, proving, proved, proven) If you prove that something is true, you show by means of argument or evidence that it is definitely true.

R

race /reɪs/ – (races) A race is one of the major groups into which human beings can be divided according to their physical features, such as the color of their skin.

reasonable /rizənəbəl/ – If you think that someone is fair and sensible, you can say that they are reasonable.

recover /rɪkʌvər/ – (recovers, recovering, recovered) When you recover from an illness or an injury, you become well again.

recovery /rɪkʌvəri/ – (recoveries) If a sick person makes a recovery, he or she becomes well again.

repay /rɪpeɪ/ – (repays, repaying, repaid) If you repay a debt, you pay back the money that you owe to someone. If you repay a favor that someone did for you, you do something for them in return.

revenge /rɪvɛndʒ/ – Revenge involves hurting or punishing someone who has hurt or harmed you.

reward /rɪwɔrd/ – (rewards) A reward is something that you are given, for example because you have behaved well, worked hard, or provided a service to the community.

S

scream /skrim/ – (screams, screaming, screamed) When someone screams, they make a loud, high-pitched cry, for example, because they are in pain or frightened. If you scream something, you shout it in a loud, high-pitched voice.

sentence /sɛntəns/ – (sentences, sentencing, sentenced) When a judge sentences someone, he or she states in court what their punishment will be.

servant /sɜrvənt/ – (servants) A servant is someone who is employed to work at another person's house, for example, as a gardener.

shade /ʃeɪd/ – Shade is an area of darkness under or next to an object, such as a tree, where the sunlight does not reach.

shelter /ʃɛltər/ – (shelters) A shelter is a small building or covered place which is made to protect people from bad weather or danger. If a place provides shelter, it provides you with a place to stay or live, especially when you need protection from bad weather or danger.

shore /ʃɔr/ – (shores) The shores or shore of an ocean, lake, or wide river is the land along the edge of it.

sled /slɛd/ – (sleds) A sled is an object used for traveling over snow. It consists of a frame which slides on two strips of wood or metal.

sorrow /sɒroʊ/ – (sorrows) Sorrow is a feeling of deep sadness or regret. Sorrows are events or situations that cause deep sadness.

spirit /spɪrɪt/ – (spirits) A person's spirit is the non-physical part of them that is believed to remain alive after their death. A spirit is a ghost or supernatural being.

stream /strim/ – (streams) A stream is a small, narrow river. A stream of things is a large number of them occurring one after another.

struggle /strʌgəl/ – (struggles, struggling, struggled) If you struggle when you are being held, you twist, kick, and move violently in order to get free.

stupidly /ˈstuːpɪdlɪ/ — If you say someone is doing something stupidly, you mean they are showing a lack of good judgment or intelligence and they are not at all sensible in what they are doing.

surround /səˈraʊnd/ — (surrounds, surrounding, surrounded) If a person or thing is surrounded by something, that thing is situated all around them.

T

throat /θrəʊt/ — (throats) Your throat is the back of your mouth and the top part of the tubes that go down into your stomach and your lungs. Your throat is also the front part of your neck.

thud /θʌd/ — (thuds, thudding, thudded) A thud is a dull sound, such as the sound a heavy object makes when it hits something soft. If something thuds somewhere, it makes a dull sound, usually when it falls onto or hits something else.

thunder /ˈθʌndər/ — Thunder is the loud noise that you hear from the sky after a flash of lightning, especially during a storm.

trial /ˈtraɪəl/ — (trials) A trial is a formal meeting in a law court, at which a judge and jury listen to evidence and decide whether a person is guilty of a crime.

U

ugliness /ˈʌɡlɪnəs/ — The ugliness of someone or something refers to its unattractive and unpleasant state.

V

victim /ˈvɪktəm/ — (victims) A victim is someone who has been hurt or killed.

voyage /ˈvɔɪɪdʒ/ — (voyages) A voyage is a long journey on a ship or in a spacecraft.

W

wave /weɪv/ — (waves) A wave is a raised mass of water on the surface of water, especially the ocean, which is caused by the wind or by tides making the surface of the water rise and fall.

wealth /welθ/ — Wealth is the possession of a large amount of money, property, or other valuable things.

wedding /ˈwedɪŋ/ — (weddings) A wedding is a marriage ceremony and the party or special meal that often takes place after the ceremony.

witness /ˈwɪtnɪs/ — (witnesses, witnessing, witnessed) A witness to an event, such as an accident or crime, is a person who saw it. If you witness something, you see it happen. A witness is someone who appears in a court of law to say what they know about a crime or other event.

wound /wuːnd/ — (wounds) A wound is damage to part of your body, especially a cut or hole in your flesh which is caused by a gun, knife, or other weapon.

A Brief Biography of Mary Shelley

Mary Shelley was born Mary Wollstonecraft Godwin in London on August 30, 1797. Her parents were famous philosophers, writers, and intellectuals. Her mother, Mary Wollstonecraft, was the author of *A Vindication of the Rights of Woman*. This important, early feminist book encouraged women to think and act for themselves — as equals with men. William Godwin was respected in England for his influential social and political ideas.

Wollstonecraft died ten days after Mary was born. William Godwin married his neighbor, Mary Jane Vial (Clairmont), when Mary was four years old. This marriage gave Mary and her older half-sister, Fanny, a mother, a stepbrother, and a stepsister. William and his new wife had a son in 1803.

Mary Wollstonecraft Godwin's remarkable background allowed her to appreciate modern ideas and gave her the chance to meet important people such as the English poet Lord Byron. She did not receive a formal education; she was taught to read and write at home. Her father encouraged her to be creative from an early age, and she was allowed to use her father's extensive library. She was also allowed to listen to the political, philosophical, scientific, and literary discussions of her father and his friends such as

National Portrait Gallery, London

the poets William Wordsworth and Samuel Taylor Coleridge.

Among the important literary figures Mary met was Percy Bysshe Shelley, a famous young poet. Percy was nineteen years old and had already been expelled from Oxford University. His relationship with his own family was troubled. Yet Percy greatly admired William Godwin. Percy, his young wife, Harriet Shelley, and his sister-in-law, Eliza, began spending time in

the Godwin home. Soon afterward, Mary and Percy began a relationship although Mary's father had forbidden them to meet.

When Mary was only sixteen years old, she and Percy ran away together to travel in France, Switzerland, and Germany. The young lovers took Mary's stepsister, Claire, with them but left Percy's pregnant wife, Harriet, behind. Mary and Percy's affair soon became strained because of Harriet's demands which worsened after they returned to London. By now, Mary was also pregnant. However, in 1816, Harriet drowned herself in the Serpentine River in Hyde Park in London. To the outrage of polite society, Mary Wollstonecraft married Percy Shelley two weeks later, on December 30, 1816, at St. Mildred's Church in London. Fortunately for the couple, Percy inherited his grandfather's estate, which freed them from the financial pressure they had previously experienced.

Mary and Percy's relationship was not only romantic but also literary. He edited the manuscript for *Frankenstein*, which Mary had begun while they were in Switzerland, and he also wrote the preface. *Frankenstein* was eventually completed in May 1817, but it was not published until January 1, 1818, when it became an instant bestseller. However, even then, Mary was not named as the author, and many people incorrectly believed that it was written by Percy Shelley. This was because the book was dedicated to William Godwin, whom everyone knew that Percy greatly admired. In fact, *Frankenstein* was not published in Mary's name until 1831. Tragically for Mary, many terrible events occurred while her novel was successful. From 1815 to 1819, three of her four children died as babies. The Shelleys moved to Florence, Italy, in October 1819. In May 1822, they moved to La Spezia. There, on June 16, Mary and Percy's fifth child died before it was born. Barely a month later, Percy drowned off the shore of Tuscany. At 25, Mary was already a widow and single mother.

Mary and her only surviving child, Percy Florence, left Italy in the summer of 1823 and returned to England. Always resourceful, Mary edited her husband's poetry and prose and published his *Posthumous Poems* in 1824 and his *Poetical Works and Letters* in 1839. Mary Shelley did not remarry; instead, she dedicated the rest of her time to her own writing. *Valperga* was published in 1823; *The Last Man* in 1826; *The Fortunes of Perkin Warbeck* in 1830; *Lodore* in 1835; and *Falkner* in 1837. However, none of her later works are as well known or as influential as her first novel, *Frankenstein*.

Starting in 1839, serious illness plagued Mary. She lived to see her only child, Percy Florence, marry in 1848. Mary Wollstonecraft Shelley died on February 1, 1851, at 53. The cause of death is recorded as "disease of the brain — supposed tumor in left hemisphere of long standing." She is buried next to her parents at St. Peter's Church in Bournemouth.

Character Summary

Victor Frankenstein

The main character and narrator of most of the story. Victor begins the story as an innocent youth fascinated by scientific discovery. By the end, he is a broken man, torn by grief and guilt. While studying at the university, Frankenstein discovers the secret of life. He creates an intelligent but horrifying monster. However, he instantly regrets his creation and tries to hide from his mistake. He keeps his monster a secret. Soon, it becomes obvious to everyone that Frankenstein cannot stop his monster from ruining his life and the lives of the people he loves.

Frankenstein's Monster

Formed from parts of dead bodies, the monster is Victor Frankenstein's extremely tall, very strong, and terrifyingly ugly creation. Although he is strong, Frankenstein's monster has the mind of a newborn baby. Sensitive and smart, the monster tries to join human society, but every human he meets is afraid of him. At first, he feels alone and abandoned. Soon, however, he feels angry and seeks revenge.

Elizabeth Lavenza

An orphan adopted by the Frankenstein family. She is almost the same age as Victor, and they are very close as children. For most of the novel, Elizabeth waits patiently for Victor while taking care of his younger brothers, Ernest and William. Eventually Elizabeth and Victory marry.

Robert Walton

The Arctic traveler. Walton's letters begin and end the story of *Frankenstein*. Walton rescues Victor Frankenstein from the ice and nurses him back to health. As Frankenstein recovers, he tells Walton his story. Walton narrates the incredible tale in a series of letters to his sister, Margaret Saville, in England.

Henry Clerval

Victor Frankenstein's cheerful childhood friend. Clerval helps Victor recover his health after creating the monster. Clerval also begins to study science and travels with Frankenstein.

Alphonse Frankenstein

Victor's father. Alphonse is very sympathetic toward his son and tries to teach him good values. Alphonse consoles Victor when he's in pain and encourages him to remember the importance of family.

Caroline Frankenstein

Victor's mother. After her father dies, Caroline is taken care of by, and later marries, Alphonse Frankenstein. She has three sons and adopts a daughter. She dies of scarlet fever, which she catches from her adopted daughter, Elizabeth, when Victor is seventeen.

Character Summary

William Frankenstein

Victor's youngest brother. The monster strangles William in the woods outside Geneva because he wants to hurt Victor. William's death burdens Victor with immense guilt about creating the monster.

Ernest Frankenstein

Victor's brother who was born in Geneva and taken care of by Elizabeth after their mother dies.

Justine Moritz

A young girl who works for the Frankenstein family. Justine is blamed for William's murder. Although she is innocent, Justine is executed which makes Victor feel even worse.

The De Laceys

A family of peasants. Monsieur De Lacey lives with his son, Felix; daughter, Agatha; and Felix's lover, Safie. Frankenstein's monster teaches himself to speak by observing the De Laceys. The monster desperately wants to be friends with them. However, when he meets them, they are scared of him and chase him away.

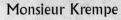

Monsieur Waldman

A professor of chemistry. Waldman encourages Victor's interest in science. He understands Victor's interest in a science that can explain the unexplainable, such as "the origins of life."

Monsieur Krempe

A professor of natural science. Krempe dismisses Victor's study of chemistry as a waste of time. He encourages Victor to begin new studies.

Mr. Kirwin

The magistrate who accuses Victor of Henry's murder.

Frankenstein: Context

Key Facts

- Full title: *Frankenstein; or, The Modern Prometheus*
- Author: Mary Wollstonecraft Shelley
- Type of work: Novel
- Genre (type of writing): Gothic science fiction
- Time and place written: Switzerland (1816) and London (1816–1817)
- Date of first publication: January 1, 1818
- Tone: Romantic, emotional, fatalistic
- Setting: Geneva, Switzerland; the Swiss Alps; Ingolstadt, Germany; England; Scotland; Ireland; the northern ice in the 18th century

"How I, then a young girl, came to think of ... so very hideous an idea?"

In the summer of 1816, Mary Wollstonecraft Godwin, a well-educated young woman from England, traveled with Percy Bysshe Shelley, her married lover, to the Swiss Alps. Unusual for that time of year, rain kept them indoors. There, along with their friend the scientist and poet John William Polidori, they entertained themselves by reading old German ghost stories. The couple's neighbor and friend, the well-known poet Lord Byron, held a competition to see who could write the best ghost story. Shelley wrote a story based on his life experiences; Byron wrote a bare fragment of a novel; and Polidori is believed to have begun *The Vampyre*.

At first, Mary did not have any ideas, but she was nevertheless determined to write a story which would "speak to the mysterious fears of our nature, and awaken thrilling horror — one to make the reader dread to look [a]round, to curdle the blood, and quicken the beatings of the heart." During one of the group's gatherings that summer, they debated the nature and origin of life. They discussed whether modern science would ever discover the origin of life. Such conversations considerably affected Mary. Not long afterward, Mary imagined the birth of a horrifying, human-made man, who was created almost as one would create an engine. Mary's story had started: the monster had his creator.

By the end of the summer, Mary Wollstonecraft Godwin won the prize in Byron's competition. She had created a terrifying story that was to become a bestseller in her own time and a classic that still affects readers nearly two centuries later.

Frankenstein: Plot

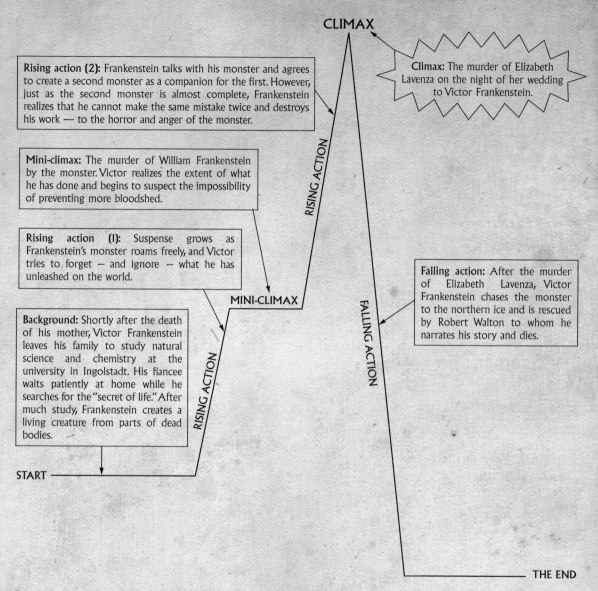

CLIMAX

Rising action (2): Frankenstein talks with his monster and agrees to create a second monster as a companion for the first. However, just as the second monster is almost complete, Frankenstein realizes that he cannot make the same mistake twice and destroys his work — to the horror and anger of the monster.

Climax: The murder of Elizabeth Lavenza on the night of her wedding to Victor Frankenstein.

Mini-climax: The murder of William Frankenstein by the monster. Victor realizes the extent of what he has done and begins to suspect the impossibility of preventing more bloodshed.

Rising action (1): Suspense grows as Frankenstein's monster roams freely, and Victor tries to forget — and ignore — what he has unleashed on the world.

RISING ACTION

MINI-CLIMAX

Falling action: After the murder of Elizabeth Lavenza, Victor Frankenstein chases the monster to the northern ice and is rescued by Robert Walton to whom he narrates his story and dies.

FALLING ACTION

Background: Shortly after the death of his mother, Victor Frankenstein leaves his family to study natural science and chemistry at the university in Ingolstadt. His fiancee waits patiently at home while he searches for the "secret of life." After much study, Frankenstein creates a living creature from parts of dead bodies.

RISING ACTION

START

THE END

Foreshadowing: Throughout his story, Victor uses words such as "fate" and "omen" to hint at the tragedy that will come. Occasionally he pauses while telling his story as frightening memories come flooding back to him.

Primary narrator(s): Robert Walton quotes Victor Frankenstein's first-person narrative in his letters; Victor, in turn, quotes the monster's first-person narrative.

Secondary narrator(s): Elizabeth Lavenza and Alphonse Frankenstein narrate parts of the story through their letters to Victor.

Point of view: The point of view shifts from Robert Walton to Victor Frankenstein, to Frankenstein's monster, and then back to Walton. Elizabeth's and Alphonse's points of view also are occasionally heard.

Hero and villain: Victor Frankenstein is both a classic mad scientist, crossing moral boundaries without concern, *and* a brave adventurer who travels into unknown scientific lands and is not held responsible for the consequences of his explorations.

Themes: The danger and responsibility of knowledge; the wonder and beauty of nature; the moral lesson that pride must have its fall; monstrosity* and secrecy

Symbols: Fire, light

* If you describe something as monstrous, you mean that it is very shocking or unfair.

Notes

Notes

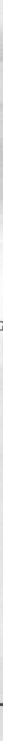

OTHER CLASSICAL COMICS TITLES

Henry V

Macbeth

Great Expectations

Jane Eyre